Bloomsbury CPD Library: Independent Learning

Dr John L. Taylor

B L O O M S B U R Y

LONDON • OXFORD • NEW YORK • NEW DELHI • SYDNEY

Bloomsbury Education
An imprint of Bloomsbury Publishing Plc

50 Bedford Square   1385 Broadway
London   New York
WC1B 3DP   NY 10018
UK   USA

www.bloomsbury.com

BLOOMSBURY and the Diana logo are trademarks of Bloomsbury Publishing Plc

First published 2018

A catalogue record for this book is available from the British Library.

Library of Congress Cataloguing-in-Publication data has been applied for.

ISBN:
PB: 978-1-4729-4581-5
ePub: 978-1-4729-4579-2
ePDF: 978-1-4729-4582-2

2 4 6 8 10 9 7 5 3 1

Typeset by Integra Software Services Pvt. Ltd.
Printed and bound by CPI Group (UK) Ltd, Croydon CR0 4YY

This book is produced using paper that is made from wood grown in
managed, sustainable forests. It is natural, renewable and recyclable.
The logging and manufacturing processes conform to the
environmental regulations of the country of origin.

To find out more about our authors and books visit www.bloomsbury.com.
Here you will find extracts, author interviews, details of forthcoming
events and the option to sign up for our newsletters.

Contents

Acknowledgements

The ideas in this book have been developed as a result of many conversations with colleagues and from shared tips about what actually works in the classroom. I'm especially grateful to those with whom I've had the privilege of working in recent months at Cranleigh School. Thanks to Martin Reader, Dave Boggitt and my other colleagues on Cranleigh SMT for encouraging the development of a 'Cranleigh Thinking' approach to independent learning. At points in this book I've included specific ideas I've picked up from Kate Cheal, Laura Dixon, Rob Lane, Adam Rothwell, Kath Skillern, Chris Stearn and Elizabeth Swinbank; I'm grateful to them. Thanks as well to Michael Wilson, Sarah Awwad and colleagues at Cranleigh Prep School, who are enthusiastically embracing and developing Socratic dialogue and project learning at the foundational stage, and to Rory Gallagher at Cranleigh Abu Dhabi for some really stimulating conversations about the themes of this book. I'm very grateful to Holly Gardner for being an understanding, astute and wonderfully facilitating editor, to Sarah Findlater for her helpful suggestions and to both of them for their provision of the series framework.

Finally, my thanks go to Georgina, Edward and Charlotte, for their patience, encouragement and support. This book is dedicated to them.

How to use this book

The Bloomsbury CPD Library provides primary and secondary teachers with affordable, comprehensive and accessible 'do-it-yourself' continuing professional development. This book focuses on learning how to teach students to think for themselves and so become more independent learners.

The book is split into two halves: Part 1 Teach yourself and Part 2 Train others.

Teach yourself

This part of the book includes guidance about what you need to improve independent learning in your classroom and school. It is split into four stages:

Stage 1: Assess

We begin with a brief exploration of what we mean by 'independent learning' and a self-assessment questionnaire designed to help you begin the process of reflecting on your own approach to independent learning and how it can be developed.

Stage 2: Improve

Stage 2 provides a summary of what researchers have found about independent learning, an overview of the main strategies for incorporating it into our classroom practice and lots of practical suggestions for actually getting it working.

Stage 3: Evaluate

In stage 3, we pause to evaluate changes that we've begun to make in our own approach to independent learning and consider what the next steps for development might be.

Stage 4: Excel

We conclude this part of the book by looking at how we can draw up a school-wide strategy for development, focusing on the approach I call 'pedagogical audit'.

This comprehensive self-teach guide also includes teaching tips, pause and think features, to do lists at the end of each chapter and recommendations for how you can share your ideas and practice with other teachers in your school and beyond. A further reading recommendation or title to discuss in a CPD reading group is also included as well as a useful blog post to read in Bloggers' corner.

By the end of part 1 you will have assessed, improved and consolidated your own approach to the development of independent learning.

Train others

Now that you are an expert in independent learning, it's time to train others in your school! External training can be expensive and in-house training is hugely valuable as it can be made relevant to your training context – the teachers and children in your school. Whether it is a quick 15-minute training session or one-hour twilight sessions, there are training plans and advice in this section to help you get started, plan and implement independent learning training in your school. This section includes:

- advice for running good CPD
- training plans for twilight training sessions, a CPD day on pedagogical audit and a series of quick 15-minute departmental CPD sessions
- detailed session and preparation notes for a full set of training PowerPoints, which can be downloaded from the online resources that accompany this book, here: www.bloomsbury.com/CPD-library-independent-learning.

See page 134 for an overview of the training plans.

Good luck with teaching yourself and training others! Keep us updated on your progress by tweeting using #BloomsCPD

Part 1

Teach yourself

1

What's it all about?

What is independent learning?

It's an odd way to begin a book on the subject, but there is no doubt about it. The phrase 'independent learning' is a trouble-maker. It makes people think silly thoughts, such as 'I can leave children to get on with their own work and they'll learn perfectly well without me' or 'Really the most important thing the teacher can do is to get out of the way of the learning' or even 'You know what I think? No one can really teach anyone anything'.

This *laissez-faire* model has tarnished the reputation of independent learning. So we need to be quite clear at the outset that independent learning does not mean lazy teaching. Sorry about that if you thought that this book was going to make it easy for you to put your feet up in the classroom. I'm not here to offer an easy ride. This book isn't a guide for lazy teachers.

Well, if not lazy teaching, then what does all the talk of independent learning amount to? What does it really mean? What marks it out? We need to be clear about this, because a fair amount of what passes for 'independent learning' is of dubious value and some versions have quite rightly been criticised. We need to separate the wheat from the chaff, so a good question to ask is: what does the genuine article look like? What really is independent learning?

As soon as we ask this question we find a potentially bewildering array of options in front of us. I've put my list – the result of just a few minutes' thought – below. You can probably think of others to add.

Pause and think

Take a moment to reflect and ask yourself, how would you define independent learning? Here are some suggestions to stimulate thought:

- children teach other children whilst the teacher puts the kettle on
- when learning takes over from teaching
- students take responsibility for their own learning
- learning to think for yourself
- learning to learn
- learning through discovery
- inquiry-based learning
- project-based learning

- active learning
- flipped classrooms
- dialogue not monologue
- anything we do in the classroom that isn't direct instruction
- all of the above? Okay – but which would you say was most important?

For me, there is something to be said for each of these concepts of independent learning though we need to be careful about what we read into them (and the kettle is definitely pushing it a bit). I am going to suggest that out of all the possible ingredients – self-direction, the transfer of responsibility, inquiry, discovery, active learning, meta-cognition – the really crucial element is *thinking*. If I was ranking the definitions in the list above in order of importance, this would be my number one. Independent learning means learning to think for yourself.

I put the emphasis on thinking not because I think the other elements don't matter but because if we get this bit right, everything else falls into place. Take, for example, the vexed and heated debate between advocates of independent learning and defenders of direct instruction. I see no need to take sides. We can have both. Here is one utterly obvious way of linking them: use direct instruction to teach students to think better and thus become more independent. Direct them to think for themselves.

In fact, as we'll see, there is a balance to be struck and getting this balance right is really important. The skill of independent learning isn't innate. Mildly paradoxical though it may sound, students need to be taught to be independent. Understanding this point is vital in separating a sensible, valuable and workable model of independent learning from the silly, cheap and unworkable versions.

As I was saying, learning to think is what really matters. Other things on the list are great if they help achieve this – less so if they don't. Projects, discovery-based learning, inquiry-based learning, dialogue – all these can be wonderful or, frankly, useless as ways of achieving independent learning. It all depends on whether doing these activities helps students learn to think. This is why I put learning to think top of my list. It is the vital ingredient.

Another reason for placing the emphasis on thinking is that educational research shows this element to be of vital importance to all learning. In his inaugural lecture given at Durham University in 2013, Professor Robert Coe put it this way: 'Learning happens when people have to think hard.'

No apologies for the fact that I'll repeat this point several times in the coming chapters. It is vital. The way to get independent learning to work in your classroom is to stimulate students to think for themselves about what they are learning. Passive students, sitting quietly, perhaps even listening carefully but not really thinking about what they are hearing, will not be learning much at all. Students who are turning ideas over in their mind, trying to connect them up with other things they have been taught, asking their own questions – these students are the ones who are likely to be learning. Why? I think you know – they'll be learning because they are thinking for themselves.

Won't results suffer?

I expect most teachers would agree with the ideal of independent learning. We all sign up, in theory at least. But let's face it, there's an awful lot of what we do in the classroom that has a much less lofty aim. It's about grinding through the syllabus, and preparing with ever-increasing precision for those examination hoops to be jumped neatly.

We're not really comfortable about this, but hey, teaching-to-the-test does get the results, and there's just so much of the syllabus to get through – independent learning sounds wonderful but where am I going to find time to fit it in? I guess most teachers look on independent learning as a friendly but distant elderly relative: good to have a visit every now and then but not every day, thanks.

I sympathise with the pressure that teachers feel under, when so much weight nowadays is placed on 'getting the grades'. But I am going to suggest that this issue is a red herring. If we approach independent learning in the right way, it is not an alternative to preparing students to face tests; on the contrary, since it is all about teaching them to think better, it can do nothing but help when the tests come around.

Wonderful though independent learning may sound, no one will be persuaded to move in this direction if they are worried that results will suffer. Thankfully, once we've understood that the heart of independent learning is getting students thinking, and that this is really just the essence of good teaching, we will see that these fears are misplaced.

I've got a lot to do – is it worth making the effort?

There are two reasons why it matters that we take time to work out how we can help students learn independently. The first is that it is much more rewarding, both for you the teacher and for your students. Independent learning is enjoyable. The second is that it works better, because students remember more. Independent learning is memorable.

Let's start – why not? – with the enjoyment factor. Speaking for myself, I much prefer lessons where my students are actively involved in discussion, debate, inquiry, project work or frankly any sort of activity more engaging than sitting silently listening to me waffling on; and from time to time my students tell me they do too.

I don't think I'm alone in this. I think many teachers feel that the lessons where there has been lively discussion and real thinking about challenging questions are the most satisfying of all. I asked my 11-year-old son about it recently and he put it this way: 'I enjoy lessons where we just think'.

Think for a moment about the most memorable lesson you have taught in the past few months. What made it memorable? The chances are that something happened to spark interest and enthusiasm; instead of rows of silent faces awaiting your wisdom, suddenly, the students were alive, alert, questioning, wanting to know. Ideas were flying about – young minds were whirring – and it felt like the lesson had sprung into life.

I think that we owe it to ourselves and our students to put a bit of work in to make more lessons like this. I also think that we stand a better chance of having engaged, interested, enthusiastic students if we create some more room for independent learning.

Pause and think

Try Googling 'Why are students bored in school?' and 'What makes a lesson enjoyable?' What results do you get?

- How serious do you think the problem of student boredom is?
- What types of lesson bore students and what do they enjoy doing?
- How important is enjoyment as a criterion of success in a lesson?

- Is it true that students are more likely to enjoy lessons where they have some degree of control over the choice of activity?
- Is it more important to give students choice or focus on trying to make the prescribed syllabus material interesting?

I don't think by any means that only enjoyable lessons are good ones. Sometimes there are things we just have to get through. We and the students need a bit of grit. But woe betide us if none of our lessons are enjoyable. Sometimes – often – we should let students enjoy exploring the world of ideas, even if this means lifting our eyes from the next learning objective in the syllabus.

Independent learning, in the right proportion, as part of the varied diet we provide for our students, helps to reinvigorate the learning process. Time spent here is time well-spent, especially if it helps to restore our students' flagging enthusiasm.

As you will appreciate, I'm not suggesting that the focus of every lesson should be on independent learning. If the first rule of good teaching is that enjoyable lessons are more likely to be memorable, the second is that variety is the spice of life. Whilst I am hugely in favour of project work, inquiry, dialogue, discussion and debate, I would by no means advise turning every lesson over to the same format. Rather, I'll be suggesting that we add independent learning to our toolkit of approaches and bring it out as and when it looks likely to help with the job at hand.

The second reason we should care about independent learning is that it leads to better quality learning. Things that we have asked about, thought about, worked on for ourselves – these are the things we tend to remember. Independent learning is memorable.

We've heard from Professor Coe that learning happens when people have to think hard, and I've suggested that the essential element in making a success of independent learning is using it to do just this: to get students thinking hard. The connection between thinking and learning is also made in an elegant one-liner by Professor Daniel Willingham, in his discussion of what improves a student's memory: 'memories are formed as the residue of thought'. What the cognitive psychologists of education are telling us is that our students are far more likely to remember what we are trying to teach them if, during the learning process, they spend time thinking about it for themselves.

If there has been no more mental activity than 'listening as the teacher drones on' then we can be fairly confident that retention levels will be low. Learning that happens as a result of thinking is more likely to stick. The trick is to create space and time for students to think things through for themselves and, whilst they are doing this, teach them a bit about how to think better. Pretty much everything you will read in this book is devoted to how we pull this trick off.

Chapter 1 takeaway

Teaching tip
How do you teach?
Reflect on a lesson you have taught recently. To what extent would you say that you encouraged independent learning and thinking during the lesson? Could you have improved the lesson by creating more opportunities for this?

Pass it on
Sharing ideas within your school
Ask colleagues for their reactions to Robert Coe's statement: 'Learning happens when people have to think hard.' Discuss whether putting the focus on thinking is a good way to improve learning. What does it take to make this happen? If this isn't happening, why not?

Colleague catch-up
Start conversations with colleagues about how they understand independent learning and about the challenges we all face in implementing it in the classroom.

Share and tweet
Share ideas about the value of independent learning using the hashtag #BloomsCPD.

CPD book club recommendation
John Dewey *Experience and Education* (see Bibliography and further reading)

Bloggers' corner
Creative Education 'Independent Learning: What role does the teacher have to play?' www.creativeeducation.co.uk/blog/independent-learning/

To DO LIST:

- ❑ Reflect on your own definition of independent learning
- ❑ Think about your own practice when it comes to encouraging students to be independent
- ❑ Discuss your feelings about making the move towards greater independence with colleagues
- ❑ Browse for blogs with discussions of independent learning
- ❑ Read John Dewey's *Experience and Education*
- ❑ Read the blog 'Independent Learning: What role does the teacher have to play?'

2 Self-assessment

This chapter is about reviewing what you already know about independent learning, what you know about the approach and what strategies you already employ. It will mirror the content of the book to come as well as touching on what is already going on in your school and classroom.

Why self-reflection?

The way we act reflects the ideas we hold but sometimes it can be difficult to spot these ideas. We find ourselves reacting to situations, or making statements, and they can come as a surprise even to ourselves. In short, all of us could do with a little more self-knowledge. The temple at Delphi, the place where the citizens of Ancient Greece went in pursuit of wisdom, contained the inscription 'know thyself'. It is good advice. By getting a clearer picture of how we think and feel about a topic, we will begin to understand why we do and say the things we do. When we know that, we are in a position to evaluate whether we are getting things right and what we need to do to change.

It is important to go through this process of self-reflective assessment, not simply to help us make progress but for the sake of those we are responsible for training or leading, or might be in the future. Unless we understand the web of ideas that surrounds us and influences our professional practice, we won't be able to make sense of the emotions – often strong ones – that surround potentially challenging and controversial ideas about learning and teaching. If we expect colleagues to develop their professional practice in the area of independent learning, we owe it to them to form a sympathetic understanding of the obstacles – real or perceived – that lie in the way.

We also need to be ready to spot the positive signs, the indications that the journey has actually already begun. A theme of this book is that independent learning is best seen not as a radical new approach that involves tearing up everything that a teacher thought they knew but as an extension of already-existing good practice. To recall what I suggested in chapter one, at its heart, independent learning involves students learning to think for themselves, and in the majority of classes, opportunities for this exist and are often taken. I'm simply suggesting we should take a look for where this is happening and then ask what we can do to make more of these openings.

How to complete the self-assessment questionnaire

On the pages that follow, there is a self-assessment questionnaire to encourage you to start the 'teach yourself' process by thinking very carefully about your current approach to independent learning before you jump into the task of trying to improve it.

When you are reviewing your practice and trying to form a clear view of where you are now and what the next steps will be, there are many ways of approaching it – your approach will depend on you as a person. For some people, it is useful to go with your gut and listen to the first thing that comes into your mind – your instinctual answer. For others, it is a better approach to spend a good deal of time really mulling over the self-assessment questions slowly and in detail.

Quick response approach

If your preference for the self-assessment is just to go with your gut, then simply fill in the quick response section after each question with the first thing that comes into your mind when you ask yourself the question. Do not mull over the question too long. Simply read carefully and answer quickly. This approach will give you an overview of your current understanding and practice regarding independent learning and will take relatively little time. Just make sure you are uninterrupted, in a quiet place and able to complete the questionnaire in one sitting with no distractions so that you get focused and honest answers.

Considered response approach

If you choose to take a more reflective and detailed approach, then you can leave the quick response section blank and go straight onto reading the further guidance section under each question. This guidance provides prompt questions and ideas to get you thinking in detail about the question being asked and is designed to widen the scope of your answer. It will also enable you to look at your experience and bring examples into your answer to back up your statements. You may want to complete it a few questions at a time and take breaks, or you may be prepared to simply sit and work through the questions all in one sitting to ensure you remain focused. This approach does take longer, but it can lead to a more in-depth understanding of your current practice, and you will gain much more from the process than the quick response alone.

Combined approach

A thorough approach would be to use both approaches together regardless of personal preference. There is clear value in both approaches being used together. This would involve you firstly answering the self-assessment quick response questions by briefly noting down your instinctive answers for all questions. The next step would be to return to the start of the self-assessment, read the further guidance and then answer the questions once more, slowly and in detail, forming more of a narrative around each question and pulling in examples from your own experience. Following this you would need to read over both responses and form a comprehensive and honest summary in your mind of your answers and a final view of where you feel you stand right now in your use of independent learning strategies to support teaching and learning.

This is the longest of the three approaches to this questionnaire but it will give you a comprehensive and full understanding of your current practice, thoughts and feelings in relation to the use of independent learning in schools. You may be surprised at the difference you see between the quick response and the considered response answers to the same questions.

• I have done this self-assessment before. • I only want a surface-level overview of my current understanding and practice. • I work better when I work at speed. • I don't have much time.	**Quick**
• I have never done this self-assessment before. • I want a deeper understanding of my current understanding and practice. • I work better when I take my time and really think things over. • I have some time to do this self-assessment.	**Considered**
• I have never done this self-assessment before. • I have done this self-assessment before. • I want a comprehensive and full understanding of my current understanding and practice and want to compare that to what I thought before taking the self-assessment. • I have a decent amount of time to dedicate to completing this self-assessment.	**Combined**

Fig. 1 How should I approach the self-assessment questionnaire?

Rate yourself

The final part of the self-assessment is to rate yourself. This section will ask you to rate your attitude in each of the areas that has been covered in the questionnaire, with a view to working to improve in these areas throughout the course of the book. The table below shows how the scale works: the higher the number you allocate yourself, the more strongly you feel about that area.

Rating	Definition
1	Not at all. I don't. None at all. Not happy. Not confident at all.
2	Rarely. Barely. Very little. Very unconfident.
3	Not often at all. Not much. Quite unconfident.
4	Not particularly. Not really. Not a lot. Mildly unconfident.
5	Neutral. Unsure. Don't know. Indifferent.
6	Sometimes. At times. Moderately. A little bit. Mildly confident.
7	Quite often. A fair bit. Some. A little confident.
8	Most of the time. More often than not. Quite a lot. Quite confident.
9	The majority of the time. A lot. Very confident.
10	Completely. Very much so. A huge amount. Extremely happy. Extremely confident.

Fig. 2 Rate yourself definitions

Independent learning self-assessment questionnaire

QUESTION 1: Do you enjoy letting students learn independently?

Quick response:

_____

_____

_____

_____

_____

Questions for consideration

- What do you like about letting students learn independently?
- Do you enjoy supervising the process of independent learning?
- What types of classroom activities do you particularly enjoy?

Considered response:

_____

_____

_____

_____

_____

_____

Rate yourself

QUESTION 1: How much do you enjoy letting students learn independently?

1 2 3 4 5 6 7 8 9 10

QUESTION 2: Do you feel that independent learning makes a difference to student attainment and achievement in your classroom?

Quick response:

_____

_____

_____

_____

_____

Questions for consideration

- Do you ever see students applying what they've learned about independent learning? When?
- Do you ever see a direct impact on your students' work following independent learning? When?
- Why do you think independent learning had an impact on those occasions?
- What would give more impact to independent learning?

Considered response:

_____

_____

_____

_____

_____

_____

Rate yourself

QUESTION 2: How much impact on student achievement and attainment do you feel independent learning has at the moment?

1	2	3	4	5	6	7	8	9	10

QUESTION 3: What is your general approach to independent learning?

Quick response:

_____

_____

_____

_____

_____

Questions for consideration

- Do you always approach independent learning in the same manner or do you try different approaches?
- Do you approach independent learning in a systematic, organised way, or is it more spontaneous?
- Do you try to include independent learning before, after or during other learning activities?
- Do you regard independent learning as a manageable challenge or as something beyond you?

Considered response:

_____

_____

_____

_____

_____

_____

Rate yourself

QUESTION 3: How happy are you with your approach to independent learning at the moment?

1   2   3   4   5   6   7   8   9   10

QUESTION 4: What educational research into independent learning do you know about and how does it inform or influence your practice?

Quick response:

_____

_____

_____

_____

_____

_____

Questions for consideration

- Are you aware of any research into independent learning?
- What gets in the way of reading educational research into independent learning (e.g. lack of time, interest, perceived value)?
- Have you discussed any educational research into independent learning with colleagues?
- Do you feel you should be guided by educational research in this area?

Considered response:

_____

_____

_____

_____

_____

_____

Rate yourself

QUESTION 4: How confident are you about your knowledge of educational research into independent learning?

1	2	3	4	5	6	7	8	9	10

QUESTION 5: Do you feel your views on independent learning match those of the school in which you work?

Quick response:

_____

_____

_____

_____

_____

_____

Questions for consideration

- Does your school have a policy regarding independent learning?
- What do you like about the general approach towards independent learning within your school?
- Are there points at which you find yourself disagreeing with your school's approach?
- If you were to write a whole-school policy on independent learning, what would go into it?

Considered response:

_____

_____

_____

_____

_____

_____

Rate yourself

QUESTION 5: How closely do you feel your own and your school's approaches to independent learning align?

1   2   3   4   5   6   7   8   9   10

QUESTION 6: Where do you feel your strengths lie with respect to independent learning?

Quick response:

_____

_____

_____

_____

_____

_____

_____

Questions for consideration

- What do you feel you do well when it comes to the promotion of independent learning in your classroom?
- Have your strengths developed over time?
- Have your strengths been noted by others (e.g. colleagues, students, parents)?

Considered response:

_____

_____

_____

_____

_____

_____

_____

Rate yourself

QUESTION 6: How confident do you feel about your ability to implement independent learning?

| 1 | 2 | 3 | 4 | 5 | 6 | 7 | 8 | 9 | 10 |

QUESTION 7: Where do you feel your weaknesses lie with respect to independent learning?

Quick response:

_____

_____

_____

_____

_____

_____

Questions for consideration

- What do you feel you don't do well when it comes to the promotion of independent learning in your classroom?
- Have you noticed any changes in the areas where you feel you have weaknesses?
- Are there any weak aspects of your approach to independent learning that others (e.g. colleagues, students, parents) have noted?

Considered response:

_____

_____

_____

_____

_____

_____

Rate yourself

QUESTION 7: How much consideration do you give to any weaknesses in your approach to independent learning?

1   2   3   4   5   6   7   8   9   10

QUESTION 8: What independent learning activities would you like to try that you have not already tried?

Quick response:

_____

_____

_____

_____

_____

_____

Questions for consideration

- Have you spotted a gap in your approach to independent learning that you feel needs filling?
- Is there an approach to independent learning that you have read about or observed in practice that you have not yet tried in your own classroom?
- What has stopped you trying it so far?

Considered response:

_____

_____

_____

_____

_____

_____

_____

Rate yourself

QUESTION 8: How confident do you feel about trying a new approach to independent learning?

1	2	3	4	5	6	7	8	9	10

QUESTION 9: What do your students think of your approach to independent learning?

Quick response:

_____

_____

_____

_____

_____

_____

Questions for consideration

- Have you ever spoken to your students to find out their views about your use of independent learning?
- What was their response?
- Have you made any changes in response to students' comments about the way you approach independent learning?

Considered response:

_____

_____

_____

_____

_____

_____

Rate yourself

QUESTION 9: How confident are you that you know what your students think and feel about your approach to independent learning?

1   2   3   4   5   6   7   8   9   10

QUESTION 10: What do you think students like when it comes to independent learning?

Quick response:

_____

_____

_____

_____

_____

_____

Questions for consideration

- Do students enjoy opportunities to engage in discussion and debate in the classroom?
- Do they appreciate being given more choice about the way they learn?
- Do they like lessons in which more time is allowed for thinking?
- Do they enjoy the opportunity to engage in project work?

Considered response:

_____

_____

_____

_____

_____

_____

_____

Rate yourself

QUESTION 10: How certain are you about what your students like about independent learning?

1	2	3	4	5	6	7	8	9	10

QUESTION 11: What do you think students need in order to engage successfully in independent learning?

Quick response:

_____

_____

_____

_____

_____

_____

Questions for consideration

- What preparation do students need before they are asked to learn independently?
- What support is necessary during the transition to independent learning?
- Once independent learning is underway, what support do students need in order to make progress?

Considered response:

_____

_____

_____

_____

_____

_____

Rate yourself

QUESTION 11: How confident are you that you know what students need in order to engage successfully in independent learning?

| 1 | 2 | 3 | 4 | 5 | 6 | 7 | 8 | 9 | 10 |

QUESTION 12: Do you know what parents and carers think about your approach to independent learning?

Quick response:

_____

_____

_____

_____

_____

_____

Questions for consideration

- Have you spoken to parents or carers about your approach to independent learning, for instance at a parents' meeting?
- What was their response?
- Have you made any changes in your approach to independent learning in response to the comments of parents or carers?

Considered response:

_____

_____

_____

_____

_____

_____

_____

Rate yourself

QUESTION 12: How confident are you that you know what parents think of your approach to independent learning?

1	2	3	4	5	6	7	8	9	10

The results

Very well done, you have self-evaluated your use of independent learning strategies to support teaching and learning and you have now taken a step towards gaining expertise in this area. You have considered your personal approach: whether you enjoy it, whether you feel you have impact, how confident you are about your understanding of the educational research, how well your views fit those of your school and department, your strengths and weaknesses, what you want to try and your students', parents', carers' and colleagues' thoughts on your approach to independent learning. It is a lot to take in so take the time to let your self-assessment sink in and reflect on it for a while.

Take a look at how you rated your answers for each question in the questionnaire and compare your ratings with the chart below. This will guide you in taking the next steps in the development of your approach to independent learning.

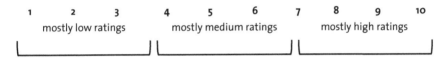

Fig. 3 How did you rate yourself?

Mostly low ratings

You have a way to go with your use of independent learning, but you are at the start of an exciting journey right now and there is huge scope for development. You have a lot to learn but there is great potential for changes that will have a positive impact on your students and improve your teaching at the same time. Now is the time to pick your first area for development and get stuck into using independent learning effectively in your classroom. One step at a time, you will develop strategies that promise to make your teaching more satisfying, enjoyable and effective.

Mostly medium ratings

You have made a start on the challenging task of implementing independent learning and you are most definitely not a novice when it comes to utilising this form of teaching and learning. However, there is still a lot you can do to enable your use of independent learning to have a greater impact on your students. Take time to prioritise the aspects of independent learning that you consider you'd most like to develop further. A focused approach will help you develop your skills and grow in confidence about your ability to embed independent learning within your classroom practice.

Mostly high ratings

You are confident about your ability to make use of independent learning as an approach within your classroom. You are in a position to begin considering the development and implementation of a training programme for colleagues straight away. At the same time, you may have identified areas where further improvement in your own practice is still possible. Stay on the lookout for ideas that you can pick up from others that will assist you in making further developments. Teaching others is an effective way of clarifying your own ideas, so as you begin to engage in the training process, expect to see changes in your understanding of independent learning.

Now what?

You have completed a full and detailed reflective examination of your own approach to independent learning. Take time now to ask what actions follow from this. If self-reflection is to be more than just a pencil-and-paper exercise, it needs to become the basis for action. Ask yourself: given what I've discovered so far about my attitudes, what steps should I be taking? Of the various things you could do, which would you say is the most important?

Chapter 2 takeaway

Teaching tip
Begin with what you are already doing
The approach to independent learning that I'm advocating is an evolutionary one. We begin with our current classroom practice, identify the points where we do already encourage independence, and then seek to move forward from these. Don't therefore be too self-critical as a result of this exercise in self-reflection. Resolve to start with what you are already doing and progress from there.

Pass it on
Work together
This chapter has been all about self-reflection, but the questions in the questionnaire are ones that could form the basis of a valuable professional development dialogue with a trusted colleague. Think about sitting down with someone you know who is also keen to develop their approach to independent learning and use some of the questions as a starting point for a conversation about how each of you can move forward.

Share and tweet

Share ideas that have emerged whilst doing this questionnaire on Twitter using the hashtag #BloomsCPD.

CPD book club recommendation

Guy Claxton, *What's the Point of School? Rediscovering the Heart of Education* (see Bibliography and further reading)

Bloggers' corner

Carl Hendrick, 'What do we mean by Independent Learning?' http://learning.wellingtoncollege.org.uk/what-do-we-mean-by-independent-learning/

TO DO LIST:

- ❑ Complete the self-assessment questionnaire.
- ❑ Decide which areas you need to work on in light of the results of the questionnaire.
- ❑ Tweet ideas that have occurred to you during the self-reflection process, using the hashtag #BloomsCPD.
- ❑ Discuss the questionnaire with a colleague.
- ❑ Keep on the lookout for blogs and books with encouraging accounts of how independent learning can make a difference.
- ❑ Read Guy Claxton's *What's the Point of School? Rediscovering the Heart of Education.*
- ❑ Read the blog post 'What do we mean by Independent Learning?' by Carl Hendrick.

3

Getting to grips with the key researchers

Independent learning: why bother?

In this chapter, we will take a look at some of the research literature that relates to independent learning. I warn you in advance that the picture painted by the researchers isn't a simple one. One problem is that the phrase 'independent learning' can mean different things to different people. Another problem is that it is not clear how it should be measured. It is difficult to measure any attribute associated with the learning process and very difficult indeed when what is being considered is something as abstract as an approach to learning.

Since the picture is complex, we should be wary of people who claim that independent learning has been proven to be the best or that we know that direct instruction is definitely better than independent learning. Things aren't so simple.

However, the positive message from this chapter is that once we understand independent learning as an approach that begins with teaching students how to think and learn for themselves, it becomes clear that there are real benefits. A balance of instruction and independence makes intuitive sense, and happily, this is also what the educational research shows.

The principles of independent learning

With the cautionary notes duly sounded, let's take the plunge and ask what the research tells us about independent learning. There's a short answer, and a longer one. Here is the short answer:

- Unguided discovery learning doesn't work very well.
- Students need to be taught to be independent.
- Scaffolded project work can foster deep understanding.
- Asking open-ended questions makes students think.
- Students learn when they have to think hard.
- Socratic dialogue to explore conceptual understanding is educationally effective.

Let's explore these points in more detail. I'll list useful sources as we go.

Unguided discovery learning doesn't work very well

Inquiry-based learning

Names: Sharon Friesen and David Scott

What to read: Inquiry-Based Learning: A Review of the Research Literature

Where to find it: www.galileo.org/focus-on-inquiry-lit-review.pdf

---

Independent learning could be defined to mean not telling students but allowing them to discover things for themselves. Supporters of this view of learning argue that it is better to allow students to make their own findings rather than ask them to absorb knowledge 'second-hand' from a teacher. If we are keen to give independent learning a try, perhaps we should simply step aside and let students work things out for themselves? What Friesen and Scott's review of research tells us, however, is that this would be a mistake. They cite the work of a number of researchers that show that unguided discovery is not a very effective form of learning; indeed, it is less effective than 'direct instruction' – the name given to the process of presenting students with essential information.

This shouldn't be a surprise and nor should it discourage us from giving independent learning a try. What the research is telling us is that we need to construct a sensible model for independent learning and it is simply not sensible or realistic to start from the assumption that students will be able to work everything out for themselves.

The problem with unguided discovery is that students who do not have a framework of concepts and knowledge in place won't be able to make much sense of the information they acquire through the research process. They will be unable to discriminate between good and bad sources. Given the vast amount of material (we can't really call it 'information', without begging the question as to whether it is reliable) that can be uncovered at the push of a button on a search engine, the task of trying to work things out from a blank-slate starting point is potentially overwhelming to most students.

So we've already found one very important lesson from the research: don't interpret 'independent learning' to mean 'leaving students alone in the hope that they will work things out for themselves'. The evidence is that they won't manage very well if you do.

Students need to be taught to be independent

Friesen and Scott drew a positive moral from their research. If we are going to make a success of independent learning, we will need to make use of a combination of direct instruction and experimentation. As they put it,

> 'These studies do not prove that inquiry-based approaches are not effective but they do support the conclusion that inquiry requires certain instructional supports.' (p23)

The phrase that is used for instructional support of independent learning is 'scaffolding'. It is an apt metaphor. Before you can start constructing a new building, you need a supportive framework in place to allow the builders to do their work. In a similar fashion, before we ask students to get to work on the task of learning independently, we need to put in place the appropriate structures (and make sure students have the right tools in their toolkits). With the right instructional supports in place, independent learning becomes a realistic prospect. Friesen and Scott observe that problem solving, reflection, concept integration and knowledge acquisition are improved when students are provided with the appropriate scaffolding.

One way to think about the importance of prior instruction is in terms of freedom. Advocates of independent learning rightly emphasise the value of giving students freedom to make choices about their learning. However, free choice is not especially meaningful if it is not informed, which means that before asking students to choose amongst a list of options (whether this be of topics to study or techniques to apply) they need to be informed about what the options on the list really mean. If we value freedom, as I think we should, we shouldn't put it first in the order of learning. Instead, we should equip students with a framework of knowledge that will enable them to begin to make meaningful choices for themselves.

Teaching independence

Name: David Didau
What to read: Independence versus Independent Learning
Where to find it: http://www.learningspy.co.uk/literacy/independence-vs-independent-learning/

David Didau makes a cogent case for saying that students will become more independent if they are provided with the appropriate scaffolding to enable them to develop the skills and knowledge required for independent study. Independence isn't innate – it needs to be taught. When training teachers, I often make the point by asking those who have been through the mill of writing a dissertation whilst at university to remember what the process involved. Most likely, they would have worked with a supervisor who would have been directing them towards the books they needed to read and challenging them to consider particular arguments or pieces of evidence. We are talking here about students with many years more training and experience than school children – and they still need advice, guidance, direction and even instruction in order to carry out meaningful independent research. If we take things back to the stage when we are just trying to get students onto the ladder that leads to independence, it should be obvious that they will need a great deal of guidance and direction.

This is one reason why it is simply mistaken to oppose direct instruction to independent learning. What matters is that we aim to make the transition from more dependent to less dependent ways of thinking, inquiring and studying, and this will happen if we carefully plan for a phased transfer of responsibility for learning from the teacher (initially) to the student (as a goal).

Scaffolded project work can foster deep understanding

Provided we set in place a well-planned programme, with initial teaching to ensure that students possess the knowledge and skills to engage in meaningful independent inquiry, this form of learning can foster deep understanding. In their literature review, Friesen and Scott refer to a 2007 paper by Hmelo-Silver, Duncan and Chinn, which presents research suggesting that when project-based learning is based on appropriate structure (as opposed to being completely unguided), it can be a powerful and effective model for fostering deep understanding.

Scaffolded project work

Names: Cindy Hmelo-Silver, Ravit Duncan and Clark Chinn

What to read: Scaffolding and Achievement in Problem-Based and Inquiry Learning: A Response to Kirschner, Sweller, and Clark (2006)

Where to find it: http://www.cogtech.usc.edu/publications/hmelo_ep07.pdf

---

One of the great advantages of project work is that it affords time for students to think in depth about a topic, rather than, as so often happens, rushing from one task to another without fully understanding any of them. The depth of understanding is made possible by the way in which, in project work, students spend time puzzling away at the connections between ideas. They learn to find their way around, to explore the linkage of one topic to another, and to see how an idea in one domain has implications elsewhere.

This sort of open-ended inquiry is very difficult to engage in if learning is entirely determined by a bullet-pointed list of syllabus learning outcomes. Hence the great value of project work for helping students begin to make connections for themselves, apply what they have learned, and see knowledge not as a set of disconnected statements but as a coherent whole.

A nice example of this was provided by a colleague of mine in the geography department of the school where I teach. He was explaining to me that his students learn about various physical processes, such as erosion and the formation of coastlines, but it isn't until they bring these together in researching a single case study of a local area of coast that they really begin to understand. And of course, once information has been understood, it is so much easier to remember. Notice as well, by the way, that my colleague only asked his students to engage in the research task after having provided them with initial instruction – an application of the point about the importance of project work being properly scaffolded.

I can vividly recall what I learned during the projects I did at school, more so than other topics I studied. I think that this is partly because of the personally chosen nature of the projects but also because they provide a single, unified context for learning. There was a central topic being explored, or a single question being answered, and this meant it was possible to draw connections between ideas and end up with a coherent, unified piece of work. This brings us neatly to the vital importance of questions.

Asking open-ended questions makes students think

One of the main aims of this book is to persuade you – and therefore your colleagues and, eventually, your students – that there is more to learning than simply knowing the right answer. One very important point that gets forgotten when our teaching is based on the right-answer model is that answers only make sense in relation to questions. So if we want our students to learn in a more meaningful way, a good first step is to focus on asking the right questions, rather than simply telling them the right answers.

If, furthermore, we want our students not simply to learn, but to become independent learners, we need to expose them to questions that will draw them into the process of thinking for themselves. For this purpose, advocates of independent learning such as Alfie Kohn have argued that open-ended questions are particularly important.

Open-ended questions

Name: Alfie Kohn
What to read: Who's Asking?
Where to find it: http://www.alfiekohn.org/article/questions/

Alfie Kohn argues that we should not begin with a set of facts to be learned, but with big, open-ended questions, such as why it is so hard to find a cure for cancer, why people lie, or whether numbers will ever end.

The important point about these questions is that there is no simple right answer. They are open-ended, inviting students to explore, inquire, research, discuss and debate. Quite clearly, to make headway with questions like these, a lot of thinking is going to be called for. They are emphatically *not* the sort of question about which students can expect to be told the 'right answer'. Perhaps there are no right answers – but even if there are, they are not obvious. The alternative possibilities each have something going for them and it is going to take some real investigation to find out whether one answer is better than another.

The implication of Kohn's argument is that we have to move away from the 'right answer' model of learning and be prepared to explore questions where there is no right answer, or where the right answer is not going to be readily found - if, that is, we are committed to helping our students develop as independent learners and thinkers.

Students learn when they have to think hard

In cases where there is no right answer, no one can reasonably expect the teacher to provide the right answer. We don't expect, for example, that a teacher of religious studies will tell students what they ought to believe about the existence of God or the morality of euthanasia. On controversial questions such as these, we each need to think for ourselves and the teacher's job is to enable this thinking to happen in a sensitive manner, allowing space for the expression and exploration of divergent points of view. As we will see, conversations like these in which there is a contrast between differing viewpoints can be educationally rich and fertile.

But what about when there *is* a right answer? Shouldn't the teacher save time and simply tell it to the students (which is often what the students themselves want)? It is tempting to teach this way, especially when there is 'a lot of material to cover'. But will our students have learned it just because we've told it to them? Perhaps, perhaps not. It isn't so easy to tell when students are actually learning. They may be sitting still, listening attentively. They may be answering questions. They may be working hard at exercises assigned to them. All of these conditions can be met without real learning going on.

Learning and thinking

Name: Robert Coe

What to read: Improving Education: A Triumph of Hope over Experience.

Where to find it: http://www.cem.org/attachments/publications/ImprovingEducation2013.pdf

---

In his work, Professor Robert Coe has drawn attention to the problem that we can't see learning – at least, not directly. Learning is a process and the manifestation of this process is in the successful completion of tasks and solving of problems that typically lie in the future. So whilst we hope learning is going on, we are always going to be a little unsure about what is really happening inside the minds of our students. The point is often made by saying that 'learning is invisible', but it would be more accurate to say that 'learning is hidden'. It can come into view; there is such a thing as seeing that a student has learned something. But we don't see the process happening whilst it is happening.

In attempting to provide a single sentence summary (necessarily over-simplistic) of the conditions under which learning occurs, Professor Coe proposes the dictum that we met in chapter one:

'Learning happens when people have to think hard.'

Coe's point is that effective learning involves thinking. To learn is to gain knowledge, and knowledge involves reasoning. You don't truly know something unless you are able to provide a reason to support the truth of what you have learned.

The need to learn to think in this way is what makes learning an active process. As with any skill, we develop the ability through practice. We puzzle away, trying to think our way through a problem, and it is in the process of thinking hard about how to do it that we learn.

Notice that if we are thinking about what we are doing, we will be learning, even if we don't get to the right answer. One of the most important reasons for advocating independent learning is as a counter to the assumption that learning is just a matter of knowing the right answer. What matters is learning to think for yourself – and so long as you are doing this, you are learning, even if your thinking doesn't take you to the right answer.

So if we want our students to learn, we need to work out how to get them thinking hard. What is it, then, that makes students think hard? One of the most important starting points is conflict. When we are faced with disagreement between different people, we have to think: who is right? When we find that something we have just experienced seems to conflict with our prior beliefs, again, we have to think: where does the truth lie? If we are presented with a situation where there seems to be equally strong evidence for and against a statement (a paradox), we are forced to begin thinking about what the truth really is. Conflict is the grit around which the pearl of independent thought coalesces.

This, by the way, is one reason why I recommend including some philosophical questions in your teaching, since by their very nature, they defy easy answers, and there seems to be more than one equally compelling response.

Socratic dialogue to explore conceptual understanding is educationally effective

We have begun to talk about questioning, which means we have reached the right starting point for understanding how we can set our students on the path that leads to genuine independence. The model for educators who see their role as more than just information transmitters is provided by Socrates, the famous philosopher of ancient Greece, who taught his students by questioning them.

If you look at one of the dialogues that Plato wrote, in which he recorded the conversations of Socrates, you will see that he used questioning as a technique for drawing knowledge out of students. He believed that knowledge already existed within the mind (in fact, he thought that it had been present in the soul even before the moment of birth) and the right set of questions could unlock this innate knowledge.

For Socrates, learning begins with questioning and the right questions to ask are the ones that will prompt students to think their own way through a problem. It is clearly the case that if a student is led towards a moment of insight as a result of having thought about a series of questions then their knowledge and understanding will be greater and more secure. For as well as having come to know the answer, they will have been led through the thought process that supports it, and since they will have thought their way through this process, they will have acquired some understanding of how to go about the task of acquiring knowledge for themselves.

At this point, I should say that the version of Socratic questioning that I'll be advocating is not quite the same as that practised by Socrates (assuming, for the moment, that the records provided by Plato provide an accurate reflection of what he was like), for the Socratic dialogues are heavily 'teacher led'. Socrates carefully frames each successive question as part of a sequence designed to lead the student up to an 'ah-ha' moment of insight (often expressed when they come to agree with what Socrates himself believes).

There is something valuable here, namely the emphasis on learning through dialogue, and on making discoveries in response to a well-chosen question. There is also, perhaps, slightly too much emphasis on the role of the teacher, who has to do most of the hard thinking when they carefully select all the questions.

We might well feel that there is something to be said for giving more responsibility for the process of inquiry to the students; that the dialogue should be more democratic. To mark this slight change of emphasis, then, I will usually speak not of *Socratic questioning* but of *Socratic mentoring*: a process in which the teacher acts, as Socrates did, as a source of questions, not answers, and in which it is expected that students will think their way through a problem until they reach a point of understanding, and, at times, when they will themselves take on responsibility for moving the discussion forwards.

We will explore in the next two chapters what it means in practice to act as a Socratic mentor. But it is worth noting that the methodology that goes with the idea of Socratic questioning, namely the idea of turning classrooms into 'communities of inquiry', has been shown to have beneficial effects both in terms of students' cognitive development and in terms of their personal development as individuals capable of participating well in reasoned discussion and debate.

Much of the work in this field is associated with practitioners of what has been termed 'Philosophy for Children'. In outline, a classroom Socratic dialogue takes place when a group of students, working with a teacher-facilitator, decide amongst themselves what question to investigate, perhaps following an initial stimulus (say, a text extract). They then discuss the question in a participatory manner, with the focus being on listening and responding to the ideas of others, and paying particular attention to the reasoning that is used to support points of view.

Socratic dialogue in the classroom

Names: Frank Fair, Lory Haas, Carol Gardosik, Daphne Johnson, Debra Price and Olena Leipnik

What to read: Socrates in the schools: Gains at three-year follow-up

Where to find it: http://www.ojs.unisa.edu.au/index.php/jps/article/view/1268/833

The study carried out by Frank Fair and others contains a helpful summary of other studies of the effects on cognitive development of participation in a programme of Socratic dialogues. Fair and his colleagues build on previous studies that provide evidence that such participation has significant cognitive benefits, and their research shows that these benefits were still detectable three years after the discussion programme had taken place.

It is tempting to think that the methodology of group discussion is more appropriate in the arts or humanities than in STEM subjects. In certain subjects, conversation is naturally part of the process; you can't learn a language without it, and in the humanities and arts, dialogue about different points of view concerning the value of an artistic technique or the interpretation of a text happens naturally enough, given an opportunity.

What isn't appreciated, though, is that discussion can play a central role in the 'right answer' subjects such as maths and science. If we actively encourage the expression of different points of view, the stage is set for a discussion as to which one is correct. This technique can be educationally effective even if the aim is for the class to come to appreciate the right answer. For by allowing students to explore different approaches or ideas before converging on the correct answer, they will begin to appreciate what it means to think through a problem, rather than simply being sponges that soak up the answers provided by the teacher. Furthermore, puzzle-solving is, for many children, an interesting and stimulating activity, particularly if carried out through discussion with others.

You are already using independent learning without noticing it

There is a voluminous research literature on all of the topics we have touched on and there are more topics we haven't addressed. We haven't yet explored such intriguing and important topics as assessment for learning, metacognition or the flipped classroom. I have tried to keep the focus of this brief exploration of the research literature on what I believe to be central: teaching students to think for themselves. I hope by now that you are persuaded of the value of this and can appreciate that thinking is connected to other valuable classroom activities, such as questioning, arguing, discussing and debating.

With this picture of independent learning in mind, it should also be clear that most of us do at least some of this as part of our 'ordinary' everyday teaching. Watch yourself as you teach tomorrow. I bet you'll find yourself acting Socratically, asking a sequence of questions to lead students along the path towards understanding. Notice when you ask questions that spark a sudden burst of discussion and argument. Consider the times in your lessons when students are thinking hard as they work on questions, perhaps naturally turning to their neighbours to talk through a problem. In each of these instances, insofar as students are beginning to think for themselves, or being equipped by you to do so, independent learning is either already happening or about to happen.

It is for this reason that I would argue that independent learning is really nothing more or less than good teaching: asking probing questions, stimulating students to think hard about what they are doing, allowing time for exploration of alternative possibilities, guiding students Socratically towards understanding and not just giving them the right answer but giving them the tools to explore the reasons behind the answers and generally allowing them greater freedom to explore for themselves as their knowledge grows.

We all do some of this, at least some of the time. I'm just suggesting we all do it a bit more.

Chapter 3 takeaway

Teaching tip
Asking questions that make students think
Would you say you tend to move too quickly to 'telling students the right answer'? What could you do to put more of a focus on questions rather than answers in your lessons?

Pass it on
Sharing ideas within your school
Put a question on the 'Teaching and Learning' noticeboard: 'What is the best question you asked this week?'

Colleague catch-up

Ask around the staffroom to find a colleague who regularly makes use of group discussion during their lessons. Invite yourself to observe one of the discussions and then have a chat with your colleague about how they manage the dynamics of classroom discussion.

Share and tweet

Share ideas about good research into independent learning using the hashtag #BloomsCPD.

CPD book club recommendation

Alfie Kohn's book *The Schools our Children Deserve* makes a case for a radical form of independent learning. Appendix A of his book provides extensive evidence of the effectiveness of the models he explores. See the Bibliography and further reading for details.

Bloggers' corner

Alfie Kohn's ideas are provocative and challenging. You can pick up some of his blogs here: http://www.alfiekohn.org/blog/

TO DO LIST:

☐ Jot a list of lessons you've learned from the research into independent learning.

☐ Spend a few minutes on Google Scholar looking for further research into topics such as Socratic dialogue, communities of inquiry and inquiry-based learning.

☐ Find a colleague who you know is sceptical about independent learning and ask them to explain their views.

☐ Consider whether you feel that on balance the evidence does favour independent learning.

☐ Read Alfie Kohn's book *The Schools our Children Deserve*.

☐ Take a look at Alfie Kohn's blog and read some of the entries.

4 Strategies for independent learning

How do you think of yourself? What is your job? Are you there to 'tell the students what they need to know' in order to pass the next test? Or are you a facilitator of learning? Will you have done your job adequately if they pass their tests but promptly forget it all (an experience I for one remember having)? How much responsibility do you, the teacher, have for learning, when, after all, you can't make anyone learn anything, can you? Should you be aiming to instil a lifelong love of learning along with the knowledge needed to pass the next test?

I hope that having read this far, and particularly having considered the strength of the research evidence, you will be in agreement with the statement that students learn better when we teach them to think for themselves. The next question, then, is how we go about doing this.

Where do I start?

Independent learning begins just as soon as we work out the right questions to ask: the ones that get students thinking. Asking thought-provoking questions to your students is crucial and it is definitely the right place from which to begin the journey of independent learning. But once we are on the road we will find a whole set of challenges confront us. What about the syllabus? How am I supposed to teach all this as well as teaching students to be independent learners? What of my colleagues in other subjects? Will it work there too? Does it mean something different for different subjects? How far can we go with this? Can independent learning be implemented on a school-wide basis?

I'm going to be suggesting two main tactics here. The first is to start where you spend most of your time, in your own classroom, with your normal lessons. Here, you can make a modest start, by embedding elements of independent learning as catalysts of thought. I expect you are familiar with the idea of a catalyst – a stimulating chemical that, even in small quantities, makes a reaction really fizz away. Catalysts of thought come in the form of engaging activities, puzzles, paradoxes or problems that spark a reaction in the classroom and get students thinking hard. And – a point that should now be sounding familiar – when students are thinking hard, they are more likely to be learning.

Catalysts of thought, though, can't do the whole job. The second tactic is to weave project work into the curriculum in the right place and at the right level. Learning to be an independent thinker takes time. We need to allow students to develop their skills as independent learners over longer periods, and here, as we'll see, project work wins hands-down as a setting for the development of skills in time management, research, critical thinking and meta-cognitive reflection. So we'll also be looking at ideas and techniques for incorporating project work into your teaching.

Teach students to think for themselves

I've made this point already, but I want to emphasise it since it is still commonly believed that giving students independence means leaving them to their own devices. This sort of minimally guided instruction has been found, unsurprisingly, to be ineffective (see chapter three).

Students need to be taught how to think for themselves. They need explicit guidance about what it means to engage in independent research, how to choose appropriate questions, how to carry out the research process, how to engage in argument and how to make sensible decisions between alternative ways of developing their work.

We saw in chapter three that a sensible model of independent learning takes account of the fact that students need direct instruction as well. The best model of learning is one that blends instruction and independence. We should bear in mind that we need them in different proportions at different stages of the learning process and at different levels, depending on the ability of our students.

My preferred model of independent learning begins with classroom discussion to enable the exploration of ideas, and lessons designed to develop the skills needed to engage in independent study. 'Instruction first, then independence' is the order of the day. Once the skills are in place and you have explored some ideas with your students, they are ready to have a go at working for themselves, and what this usually means is engaging in project work of some sort.

Where, then, should we start? I suggest we begin by thinking about the sort of question we ask our students.

Find the flashpoints

I began thinking about independent learning when I noticed that there are some questions that seem to work really well when it comes to getting students thinking for themselves. If, in an otherwise quiet physics lesson, I ask the question 'What is time?' I can pretty much guarantee it will ignite the lesson and lead to an explosion of excited debate. I call questions like this 'flashpoint' questions on account of their power to cause debate to break out.

Flashpoint question examples

- What makes me the person I am?
- Can animals think?
- Can a bad person produce good art?
- Can we ever translate a word perfectly from one language to another?
- Is beauty a real quality?
- Can we assign a monetary value to anything?
- What is a country?
- Is maths invented or discovered?
- Do we know what happened five minutes ago?

I think you can find flashpoint questions in pretty much any subject area. I've compiled a list here: https://www.slideshare.net/cranleighschool/cranleigh-thinking-week-1318-march

So what makes a question work as a starting point for independent learning? I think there are three key features to keep in mind when planning a scheme of work:

1. **Is the question *interesting?*** We won't get far unless the questions we ask are ones that engage our students' interest.
2. **Is it *controversial?*** There needs to be more than one possible answer and scope for argument about which answer is best.
3. **Is it *fertile?*** Will thinking about possible answers lead into research and further learning?

Let me say a little more about these points.

Interesting

In saying that a question needs to be interesting, I'm aware that there are many topics we have to teach simply because they need to be learned, regardless of whether they are particularly interesting. Fair enough – but these questions won't work as starting points for genuine independent learning. The whole point about independent learning is that the motivation for study comes from within the student and they are not going to be particularly motivated to engage in independent research into a question they find boring.

I'm not saying that everything we teach has to be immediately interesting. But I find it does help from time to time to drop some flashpoint questions into my lessons as a way of showing students just how many interesting questions there are out there. These questions are invitations to start thinking more deeply and independently.

Controversial

Flashpoint questions work because they are controversial. They are the ultimate antidote to the expectation that you the teacher will provide the right answer, since there is no right answer (or at least, none that is obvious). Flashpoint questions are starting points for argument, not instruction. When more than one answer can be given, there is room for argument about which, if any, of the possible answers is best.

The element of controversy is really important if we are going to set tasks that involve analysis and argument rather than simply gathering up lots of facts. If we want to move our students beyond thinking that learning means knowing the right answer, we have to present them with issues where there is no obvious right answer.

Fertile

The third feature of flashpoint questions is fertility. Discussion and debate are most effective when students are led to realise that in order to defend their ideas, they need to know more. Questions that initially trigger discussion and argument but then lead into a process of research and further study are the best of all.

Use flashpoint questions to generate better thinking

It is a common experience of teachers to set students project work to do, then find themselves disappointed when what comes back is a report with a bunch of facts, more or less taken directly from websites. What can we do to encourage our students to move beyond simply seeing research as a matter of gathering up bits of information? How can we encourage them to engage in analysis and evaluation?

Choosing a good question is crucially important here. Suppose you want your students to learn about self-driving cars. You've decided to set them a research assignment on the topic of the self-driving car. With that title, you'll probably get essays with a lot of facts from Google about self-driving cars.

Suppose instead that you ask the question: 'Should we allow self-driving cars on public roads?' This is a good question. It is interesting; it makes us think about what the world might be like in a few years' time, when we might find ourselves being overtaken by a driverless car. There's plenty to explore here – and, of course, plenty to argue about. There certainly isn't a simple right answer to be found.

In the process of answering the question, lots more questions are going to be raised. What are these vehicles exactly? How do they work? Is their behaviour determined by how they are programmed and what assumptions go into the programs? We have a question that is interesting, controversial and fertile – we have a good flashpoint question.

What about the 'right answer' subjects?

Please don't make the mistake of thinking that flashpoint questions only belong to the arts subjects, where there is obviously room for alternative answers. Whilst we tend to think of science and mathematics as 'right answer' subjects, there is often room for discussion, debate, argument and counter-argument and the investigation of alternative answers here as well.

I taught a physics lesson to a group of 13-year-old students recently. I put an iron rod on top of an electromagnet, dropped an aluminium ring onto the rod then turned on the power. The ring jumped into the air. That got the class interested. They got more interested when I reminded them that aluminium isn't actually magnetic. 'Why did that happen? It is up to you to find the answer and choose how to present it', I said. A few lessons of research and preparation later, and we had a whole variety of outcomes including group presentations, posters and PowerPoints.

The great thing about the problem was that there was no single right answer. There are different ways of thinking about what happens, different aspects to explore (such as why the ring also heats up) and different ways of presenting answers. We had a good flashpoint question to explore: one that was interesting, controversial (there wasn't a single obvious right answer) and fertile (students began to discover new physics that I hadn't taught them).

Discover the power of paradoxes

Suppose I say to you that you cannot move across the room, because before you move across the room, you have to move halfway across it, and before you can do that, you have to move half of halfway, and... you get the picture. It looks as though you have to do an infinite number of things to simply cross the room. You can't do an infinite number of things, can you? Yet you can cross the room. We have a paradox: an apparent contradiction (this one was discovered by the Greek philosopher Zeno of Elea).

Paradoxes work well as starter activities to get students thinking, because they create the feeling that something has to be right, but can't be right, at the same time. This is mentally uncomfortable; students often start pulling faces and saying 'this is *so* annoying'. Well, okay, I would then ask them to think their way out of the problem. If you don't like the feeling of confusion, think hard about the assumptions that go into the paradox and decide which ones might be wrong. This sort of thinking – spotting and challenging assumptions – is a vital part of deeper learning.

Effective starter activities to catalyse thinking

For a set of absolutely wonderful sources of paradoxical questions, look up the '60 second adventures in thought' series on YouTube (https://www.youtube.com/playlist?list=PL73A886F2DD959FF1).

This series features paradoxes that are excellent starting points for debate. They present arguments for and arguments against, leading to the question: what is really going on here?

Pause and think

- How often do I ask questions where there is no obvious right answer?
- Am I comfortable asking controversial questions in my lessons?
- What are the flashpoint questions in my subject area?
- What makes a question interesting?
- Of the questions that I've asked in my lessons recently, which ones were effective in helping students learn something new?

Use projects to give time for free exploration of ideas

I love those moments when a question ignites debate and the ideas and arguments start to flow. But I'm aware that excitement alone doesn't imply that there is meaningful learning going on. The challenge is to harness the burst of enthusiasm and interest that accompanies flashpoint debates and use it to power a real journey of inquiry in the form of a student project.

A project is a process and processes take time. This is both a challenge and an opportunity. It is a challenge because none of us, least of all our students, finds time management easy. It is also a challenge because time is usually in short supply – we're all aware of that long and detailed list of 'things they need to know', and unless you are in an increasingly small minority of subjects that includes project work as a requirement, finding time to fit it in alongside the formal curriculum will be tough.

It is worth making the effort, though, since students in the project process have a chance to learn really valuable skills, skills that they simply cannot acquire if all they are asked to do is short assignments or banks of exam-style questions. Through project work students can acquire qualities such as perseverance, learning from mistakes, trying ideas out and having to revise them, connecting together multiple elements to make a coherent whole, experimenting with alternative techniques and learning to cope with a series of deadlines.

As a means of helping students develop as independent learners, therefore, project work reigns supreme. The value of project work lies partly in its personal nature. A project is something that the student owns. Typically, they will have at least some choice as to the topic, ranging from selection from a list of recommended topics or titles, through to completely free choice. The starting point, the direction of development and the final shape of the work will reflect the student's own interests and priorities and even, to some extent, their own personality. The domain of project work is as wide as the world itself: there is ample scope here for the pursuit of personal interest and the satisfaction of curiosity.

Unsurprisingly, when we allow students the freedom to pursue topics that are personally interesting and meaningful to them, they tend to work better. In fact, I would go further and say that in my experience, a satisfying, personally-directed project can often be the best piece of work a student does at school. If we are serious about giving our students space to learn independently, we will need to get to grips with the challenge of project-based learning.

What is a project?

The key point is that a project isn't simply a task; it is a process. If a student works in a shop selling sportswear, they are carrying out a task. If you ask your students to design, create and sell tracksuits to raise money for charity, then we have a project.

Any project involves four main stages:

1. **Planning:** Deciding on the central question or brief for the project and working out how to address it.
2. **Researching:** Finding out about the work of other people and analysing how it relates to the project's aim.
3. **Developing:** Exploring the merits of alternative possible answers to the question or ways of meeting the brief.
4. **Reviewing:** Reflecting on the extent to which the project has met its aims and lessons learned from the process.

The scale of project work varies enormously. I sometimes set projects that take less than two weeks' work. The longest projects (extended projects) my students do take almost two years. I tend to use small-scale project work as an element within a scheme of work that is largely dominated by learning a set curriculum. Large-scale project work needs to have its own chunk of timetabled time allocated to it.

There is no right answer to the question of how long you should allocate to a project; it depends on the time that is available, the needs and abilities of your students and the learning aims you hope to achieve. Small-scale project work is good for adding variety to a scheme of work and giving students a taste of independence. Large-scale projects are a great way of getting deeper into areas such as time management, deeper research and the development of personal perspectives.

Size of projects

The model for project work that I'm describing in this chapter is designed to work over a period of several weeks or longer. I find that it is valuable to do a large-scale project with students over this sort of length of time, because it enables them to learn the skills of independent research and the investigation of argument and counter-argument. In terms of project size, if I was working with 16 to 18-year-olds, I would expect projects to end up being around 4,000 to 7,000 words in length. There is no hard and fast rule, though. The exact length depends on the type of project: practical projects often take the form of shorter reports, accompanied by a sketchbook with plans, cuttings, photographs, mind-maps, design sheets and the like. For 13- to 15-year-olds, 2,500 words is a sensible target and for younger students, 500–1,000 words.

The choice of title is all-important

You can decide how much freedom you want to give here. Sometimes – if your aim is to teach a specific skill in research, for example – you might determine the topic area for your students. Ideally, though, they should have some say in the choice of title. Perhaps you determine the overall topic (e.g. 'revolutions') and they choose a title within that topic area. If you want to allow more freedom still, it is worth putting in place some guidelines.

I usually spend a few lessons before the project begins having flashpoint discussions, hoping that students will be stimulated by these and get some promising ideas from which to begin their projects (this is admittedly a little like the 'pick a card, any card' trick – but you can be upfront with students and explain that you are discussing topics that would be good starting points for project work, as well as allowing them the scope to propose something different if they want to).

I ask students to propose their project idea formally. They should write about the rationale for their choice of question, the areas they will research and so forth. I will then have a conversation with them about the suitability of their proposed title. The really crucial elements I look for are more or less the same as those that flashpoint questions possess.

The title needs to be one they find *interesting* (otherwise, how likely is it that they will stick at the project?). A project, remember, is personal: the best projects are powered by a strong sense of personal engagement, whether because the project links to their hobbies, interests, issues that concern them, topics studied in other classes, aspirations for future work or simple curiosity.

It also needs to be *fertile*: it should lead into a process of meaningful research. A good way of checking this is to ask the student to do some initial research and identify three sources that could be used in their project. If they can, good – they are on the way. If not – perhaps the title needs to change.

I keep in mind here the level of ability of the student and the possible complexity of the topic. It is common for students to be too ambitious, as they don't appreciate the challenge of research or the level of ideas that will be involved. It is often better to go for a *simple* title.

Above all, the question or brief needs to be *open-ended*: there needs to be room to explore alternative answers or designs. A title such as 'How have Formula 1 cars developed over the past ten years?' won't work very well. A better title would be: 'Should we do more about driver safety in Formula 1?'

Write from the start

Once a rough title is in place (bearing in mind that titles often change, hopefully becoming clearer and more specific as the project develops), the next step is to begin writing the project. It may come as a surprise to students that they are expected to start writing straight away, but in my experience, this is vital.

I tell my students that the best way to write the project is to write from the start. Of course, what they write might not be very good – but they can always change it! Project work is all about momentum, and writing a little each week is a good way of keeping the momentum going.

If they are doing a practical project, it is usually a good idea to get hold of a big sketchbook, to record the journey of ideas. All too often, students doing practical work just want to get the thing done – make their music, produce their film – but it is the journey of ideas that makes a good project, and this needs to be tracked.

Provide students with the scaffolding for their project

Providing students with a template for their project work helps a great deal. For larger projects, it is helpful as it breaks down the daunting task of writing what will seem to students a huge piece of work into a less threatening set of sub-tasks (e.g. 'Write 500 words of research in the next five weeks').

There is a benefit for you the teacher too. One of the problems with managing independent learning is keeping track of the students. I solve this problem by creating a template for the project then using this to create a plan of work. I then expect students to keep in step with the plan, and provide them with guidance as they move from stage to stage.

For example, the template I use for written projects looks like this:

A template for projects

Initial plan	Choosing research question, planning areas of research.
Introduction	Explain the research question. Define key terms.
Research review	Summary of the relevant source materials.
Discussion	Point of view, argument, counter-argument, response to counter-argument.
Conclusion	Brief summary of the argument.
Evaluation	Reflection on what has been learned during the project process.
Bibliography	Full list of sources.

With this structure in mind, a plan of work can be created. Suppose I have 12 weeks available. My plan would look like this:

A plan of work for a project

Proposal stage	1 week
Research	3 weeks
Discussion	4 weeks
Conclusion and evaluation	1 week
Introduction and bibliography	1 week
Re-drafting	2 weeks

I would explain a few key points about the process to students.

Student project guide-sheet

- It is important to take time to plan carefully: don't just pick the first idea you come up with. When you think you know what you want to do, start to write the initial plan and begin researching. Remember you can change your mind if you find it isn't working well!
- Don't start with the introduction. You will probably change your question during the course of the project and until you have written the project, you won't really know what it is all about.
- Research is important. A project is not just an essay. You need to find out what other people have written about your topic. It is best to organise your research into sub-topics. Make a plan of these early on and then, as you find source material, you can slot it into the relevant section. Every time you use a source, include a citation and a brief evaluation of the source (discussing whether it is reliable or not).
- If you are doing a practical project, you will need to do technical research, look at examples of the type of thing you intend to produce and gather information about the possible materials and techniques you can use in your work.

- The discussion section is where you give your answer to the question, and give arguments to support it. The arguments should be based on the evidence you have found in the sources you look at. As well as giving supporting arguments you should put the counter-arguments – the arguments against your point of view – and say how you would answer them. Remember that the point of the discussion is not to describe what other people think – this is what you did in the research section. The point of the discussion is to get stuck into the argument and say what you believe.
- If you are doing a practical project, in the discussion section you should describe and evaluate the strengths and weaknesses of different possible ways of achieving your creative intentions.
- Write a short conclusion in which you sum up what you have argued. The evaluation of your project is the place where you think about the process: what has gone well and what has gone badly? What would you do differently next time around? What lessons have you learned from doing the project?
- The introduction should explain the question you have chosen and give the reasons why it is important. You should define any terms you will use in the project and give a brief overview of the project as a whole, saying what areas you will look into.
- If you are using Word to write your project, the computer will do all the citations and bibliography for you. Click on the 'References' tab, then 'Insert Citation', then 'Add New Source'. Type in the details of your source and the computer will generate the citation. At the end of your project, click on the 'Bibliography' tab and the bibliography will appear. If you are working on a Mac, go to 'Document Elements', click on the '+' and you will have the same options.
- Easier still, get the app called RefMe on your phone. You can generate citations by pointing your phone at a bar code or typing in a URL.
- If you are working on GoogleDocs, click on the 'Tool' bar and there is a terrific tool called 'Explore'. It creates a list of sources on the right-hand side of your screen, and if you click '+' on a source, it automatically generates a citation to the source in a footnote. You can also share your work with your teacher and they will then be able to check your progress and add comments to your work without you having to send it to them.

Be a Socratic mentor

As we have seen, Socrates taught by asking questions. According to him, teaching is neither a matter of transmission of information from the mind of the teacher to the mind of the student nor a matter of the student discovering things for themselves. Rather, it is a process in which knowledge is derived through dialogue, through question and answer, a process in which the teacher or mentor stimulates the student to think their way towards an appreciation of the truth. Understanding this process is crucial to understanding how to support students who are engaged in project work.

Once a project is underway, you should expect students to be working independently, with support from you. This is the point to use the technique I call 'Socratic mentoring': looking at the work your students have done, asking them probing questions, challenging them to research more deeply or think about specific arguments or counter-arguments. The key question to discuss with a student is: what seems to be the best step to take next? A simple question, asked at the right time, can often help a student discover the way ahead with their project.

To engage in further Socratic dialogue, it is worth gathering the group together for a work-in-progress seminar, where each student takes a few minutes to explain their work to the rest of the group, who can then offer (helpful!) comments, suggestions or questions. This is also a way of gently putting a little pressure on the less productive members of a class.

Use micro-tutorials

One of the great benefits of working on projects is that once students are underway, you can allow them to work (with some supervision) and lesson time can then be used for short individual tutorials. I try to book a computer room, or the school library, so that students have a space for working on their own, whilst I call up individual students for a one-to-one Socratic discussion about their work. Some weeks, I find all that I need to do is encourage them to keep going. Other weeks, we need more in-depth discussion, particularly if they have hit a block. With project work, momentum is all-important, so I'm constantly looking for ways to help them take the next step, perhaps by changing their title to make the project more manageable.

Be careful, though, not to overload the student with tasks. The outcome from a micro-tutorial (a three- or four-minute review of the student's work) will typically be one main target for completion during the next week or so.

During micro-tutorials the sort of questions I typically ask are:

- Can you remember what your title is?
- Have you been able to find research sources? (If the answer is no, then: should we find a different title?)
- Have you starting using the template for project work?
- Have you made a plan of areas for research?
- Have you summarised the sources in your own words?
- Have you included citations?
- Have you included some linking and topic sentences to help the reader make sense of your research?
- What do you think the answer to your question is?
- What arguments would you give?
- What are the arguments against your view?
- How would you answer the counter-arguments?
- When you are reviewing your project, being honest, where are the gaps and weaknesses?

It helps to keep track of the discussions and any targets that have been set on a supervisor's spreadsheet; this way both the teacher and the student have a reference point for future discussions.

Using IT to support independent learning

I've already mentioned the incredibly useful citations tool. Another tool I use a lot is the 'Styles' bar. You can create a template document with a series of headings and provide this to your students as a way of helping them structure their project. If you use the Styles bar and select 'Heading 1' for the main headings, then 'Heading 2' for any sub-headings, the computer will nicely stylise the headings in the document with an appropriate font. If you then go to the References bar and click 'Table of Contents' a contents page appears. This tool helps to make the project look professional from the start, and, more importantly, it helps students to organise their work efficiently.

The other IT tools I use all the time are open access sources. There are more and more of these: high-quality sources of research that can be accessed, at least by older students. If your school can afford it, you can buy access to sites that offer access to high-quality research, but there are plenty of good free sites as well. OpenDOAR and Core are excellent, as is Google Scholar. For younger children, Britannica Kids allows you to do age-specific searches.

Weblinks:
http://www.opendoar.org/
https://core.ac.uk/
https://scholar.google.co.uk/
http://kids.britannica.com/

Another tip about Google: if you click on 'Tools' when you have done a search, you can change the time setting so that the search hits are organised to show the most recent ones (e.g. in the last week or month) first. This is helpful when you are trying to find out if anything has happened recently in connection with a specific topic.

If you haven't discovered Google Classroom, I strongly recommend it. As I mentioned in the student guidance, if students log on to Google Docs and share their work with you, you will be able to log in and see what they are doing in real time, and add comments even as they work. The Google Explore Tool makes researching as easy as can be.

Also, if you want students to do group projects, you can ask one of them to start the work using a template you provide, then share it with others in the group. Each of them can then contribute to the same document simultaneously (and you can keep track as well of who has done what). As a tool for project work, this is incredibly helpful.

Sooner or later, you will need to do something about plagiarism checking. The rule here is: prevention is better than cure. Teach the students about what they can and can't do (i.e. you can't just cut and paste, but you can rewrite in your own words with a citation, or include short direct quotations). I use a plagiarism-checking program to check students' projects. I do this before the end of the project course, so that if there are problems, they can be dealt with by re-writing. You can encourage students to run a plagiarism check for themselves. There are a number of free plagiarism checkers available if you search online.

Chapter 4 takeaway

Teaching tip
Asking questions that make students think
Write a list of questions that work well at making students stop and think. Often, these will be questions where more than one answer

is possible, so that some students will think one thing and others something else. This naturally leads into discussion and debate and means that students have to think their way through the problem. You can use them in class as starters or plenaries. Remember the importance, once a question has been asked, of allowing students thinking time before they are expected to answer. Try out a Socratic dialogue in class, where you deliberately don't give answers but use a sequence of questions to lead students to the point when they grasp the answer for themselves.

Pass it on

Sharing ideas within your school

Capture a short section of a lesson by recording it and transcribing the comments. You can use this if you have a Teaching and Learning slot in a departmental meeting or in a CPD session. Use it to start a conversation about the importance of questioning and how the Socratic technique of teaching by questioning can be made to work.

Colleague catch-up

Start conversations with colleagues about their experience of valuable questions. Look for patterns. For example, there is evidence from research that asking students to give a reason for their answers using a simple 'Why?' improves their retention of what they are learning. Does this work in different subject areas? Do open questions with more than one answer work well in different subjects? Can this technique be applied even in maths, where there usually is a right answer? (I think it can, so long as students don't know the right answer to start with.)

Share and tweet

Share ideas about the value of questioning using the hashtag #BloomsCPD.

CPD book club recommendation

Read the dialogue between Socrates and Meno's slave, in which Socrates uses a sequence of questions to elicit knowledge of a geometrical formula from the slave. The dialogue is found in Plato's book *Meno* and is available online (see Bibliography and further reading). The dialogue with the slave boy begins about halfway through; search for the place where Socrates says 'Attend now to the questions which I ask him, and observe whether he learns of me or only remembers.' Don't worry if the details of the maths are hard to follow, but notice the way in which

Socrates uses questioning first to provoke his student into realising that he does not know what he thought he did, then towards discovery of the truth.

Bloggers' corner

For a stimulating discussion of open and closed questions, see Peter Worley's blog 'The Question X revisited' https://philosophyfoundation. wordpress.com/tag/closed-questions/

TO DO LIST:

❏ Think about your own preferred definition of independent learning.
❏ Notice the points in your lessons when students are made to stop and think.
❏ Draw up a list of questions that catalyse thinking.
❏ Look for opportunities to engage students in project work.
❏ Read the dialogue between Socrates and the slave boy in Plato's *Meno*.
❏ Find Peter Worley's blog about questioning and read it.

5 Putting it into practice

In chapter four, we saw how a broad strategy for introducing independent learning relies on techniques for questioning, drawing students into discussion, and exploring ideas in greater depth through project work. In the first half of this chapter, we'll look at ten specific ideas for getting independent learning going in the classroom. Then in the second half of the chapter, I will present you with strategies for incorporating the ideas into your scheme of work.

Ten strategies for implementing independent learning in your classroom

1. Open minds with open questions

We saw in chapter four that flashpoint questions where there is no obvious right answer work well as catalysts of thought. As a way of drawing students into deeper learning and thinking, I like to run starter activities that consist of discussing a deep, open-ended question. The point is to get students thinking and to show them that this is worth doing even if they don't reach an answer, because they learn better when they are thinking.

I normally ask them to discuss a question in pairs and then invite some of them to feed back to the rest of the group. This way, everyone gets an opportunity to do some thinking, even if they are reluctant to speak in front of the whole class. Below is an example of this type of activity.

Activity: Open questions, open minds

Choose one of the following questions to discuss with a partner. Be ready to share your ideas with the rest of the group.

- Could there be a science of love?
- Are numbers real?
- Am I the same person as I was when I was born?
- Should there be a single government for the whole world?
- Where do words get their meaning from?
- Why do we care about the past?
- Could you have a language without tenses?
- What makes things right and wrong?

---

2. Reorganise your classroom

We learn to think by thinking, and most of us think better when we have a chance to talk things through. If your students are going to develop into better thinkers, classroom conversation – by which I mean serious discussion of ideas, argument and debate, not just chat – is vital.

But all too often, conversation is impeded by the layout of the classroom. In the majority of classrooms, the arrangement of chairs sends a clear message: watch, learn, listen to the teacher. Sit in your rows and keep your eyes forward.

This is fine if we need the students to listen whilst we instruct them. It isn't good at all for getting meaningful classroom discussion going. Take a look at the room you teach in and ask: if I wanted to arrange it to enable discussion, what would I do?

One crucial point is that in any discussion group, everyone ought to be able to see everyone else. That pretty much puts paid to rows of desks with everyone facing forward. What alternatives are there?

Room layouts to encourage discussion

Talk to your neighbour
The quickest, easiest way of getting a discussion activity going, without any need to move the furniture, is to ask students to talk to their neighbour. This works well if you want to include short bursts of discussion during a teacher-centred lesson but it is only possible with groups of two or three.

Full circle
This is good from the point of view of allowing eye contact, and nicely democratic: there are no privileged points in the circle; everyone is equal. But it can be difficult to achieve with a large class.

Horseshoe
This can enable eye contact between everyone and makes it possible to keep a focus on the teacher/whiteboard in the centre, if you want to send a message to the class about staying focused.

Small groups
Grouping students around a small table (or tables pushed together) works well if you want small-group dialogue or problem solving. It is not ideal though if you want to hold a plenary discussion.

Fishbowl

The idea here is to use an inner ring and an outer ring. Students around the outside are expected to listen to the discussion, perhaps making their own notes and reporting back later about what they've learned. The two circles can then swap around.

The fishbowl has the advantage that you can hold discussions even with classes of up to 30, since 15 is about the largest size for a meaningful discussion. You can also get useful feedback from the outer ring students, both about what they have learned and about the discussion itself. The method does need a reasonably large room, and you'll also need to think carefully about the topic for the discussion and how to divide it into two sections.

If you are lucky enough to have a large classroom, you could set out different arrangements in different areas. The best teaching room I ever had was an old library, which was big enough to contain a horseshoe arrangement centred on the whiteboard, with space for two small groups around low circular tables off to the side. The discussion area also had soft, padded chairs, which the class adored.

But the key point is that any classroom can be adapted to make discussion flow more readily. Just remember, when planning your lesson, to think about what sort of layout will be most helpful.

3. Argumentative question-bouncing

When you get an answer from a student, it is tempting to congratulate or correct the student and move on. But if we want our students to think more deeply, we need to challenge them to think about their answers. Question-bouncing is a very effective technique for doing this.

Activity: Question-bouncing

When you get an answer, don't reply yourself but bounce the question to someone else in the group. You can do this directly ('Sarah – do you agree with what Phil said?') or by asking 'Who agrees?', 'Who disagrees' (this gets everyone in the group thinking), then inviting someone in agreement and someone in disagreement to explain their reasoning.

Having heard their answers, go back to the original student and invite them to respond. You could then have another show of hands to see if the group opinion has shifted. Often what happens is that there is a realisation that something was wrong with one of the answers, and so the class makes progress towards a better understanding of the answer.

Notice that question-bouncing works just as well regardless of whether the initial answer is right or wrong. Understanding the reasons behind the right answer is important and helps to fix it in the student's memory. So it is worth bouncing the question around the class, even if the right answer has been given, as a way of getting students to think through what it is that makes the right answer right.

4. A logical model

Logic is a wonderful tool for helping students think more clearly. Fundamentally, logic is the study of valid arguments. An argument is valid if the premises (the assumptions) support the conclusion. An invalid argument (a fallacy) is one in which the conclusion does not follow from the premises.

Logic is the framework within which thinking takes place. It can help students if we make this framework explicit.

Logic can get very complicated, but for the purposes of helping students to organise their thinking and reflect on the reasons behind their ideas, I use the following simple model, proposed by Sergia Hay (see Bibliography and further reading).

A logical model of arguments

- Point
- Argument
- Counter-argument
- Response

Logical discussions

The logical model can be used as a guide when facilitating discussion, where questions like these are helpful:

- What is your point of view?
- What argument can you give for that?
- Does anyone have a counter-argument?
- How would you answer that counter-argument?

One valuable feature of using this structure is that it helps you keep the discussion focused on a specific issue and draw out arguments for and against a specific point. Sometimes I briefly write up a statement from one of the students in the discussion and the supporting argument, which I can then invite other students to analyse and respond to.

Logical essays

The logical model can also be used by students for structuring their essays.

A writing frame for logical essays

Introduction: A statement of the question and the point of view for which they will argue.

Main section: Arguments in favour of their point of view.
Counter-arguments to their point of view.
Reponses to the counter-arguments.

Conclusion: A brief summary of the main argument for their point of view.

Using debate to develop logical skills

One activity that works extremely well for developing students' logical skills is class debate. The structure of a debate leads naturally into the construction of argument, with consideration and response to counter-argument.

It may not be possible for everyone in a class to participate as speakers, but even if they are involved in helping to plan the case for or against a proposition, they will find themselves thinking through the logic of a topic, as they will have to consider what the best arguments for their side are, as well as trying to anticipate and work out responses to the arguments from the opposing team.

I find that a class debate works really well as a strategy for getting students to focus clearly on the logical analysis of arguments, and this is a terrific thinking skill for them to develop. It also provides an opportunity for you to work with them on their oral communication skills.

5. Questioning knowledge claims

We usually take it for granted that we know things, but do we know what we think we know? How do we know? Challenging students' confident claims to know things is an effective way of getting them thinking and learning more deeply.

A conversation with Socrates tended to be challenging in just this way, since he had a tendency to ask questions designed to stop people who thought they knew the right answers in their tracks. Asking them to explain or justify what they believed often led to the realisation that they weren't so clear after all about what the right answer really was. If we are serious about turning our students into independent thinkers, it's worth following Socrates' example by challenging students to justify their answers.

I doubt that anyone would disagree about this – but in practice, it can prove difficult. We all know the experience of asking a question in class, getting the right answer, praising the student and moving on. We usually do this because we want to keep the lesson moving briskly (there's such a lot to get through). After all, if we get the right answer, that shows they know what we want them to. Or does it?

Sometimes, the right answer might be a lucky guess. Or it could be something that a student has vaguely remembered, but doesn't understand. The quality of their knowledge isn't shown by the fact that they gave the right answer. If we want to be sure that our students *really* know what they are talking about, we need to get them to take a step beyond the right answer: we need to get them thinking about why the right answer is right. We need them to give the reasons for their answer.

Beyond the right answer

Here are some good questions for getting our students to move beyond simply giving us the right answer to thinking about the reasons behind it:

- Why do you think that?
- What makes you say that?
- What reason can you give for that answer?
- What's the evidence for that?
- Can you give an argument to support that?

These questions are powerful tools for getting students to look beyond the right answer and explore the realm of reason, argument, explanation and inquiry.

As well as deepening their thinking, these questions can make learning more memorable. Even in a case of simple factual recall, it turns out that it is educationally advantageous to explore the reasons behind the right answer. Cognitive psychologists who have studied memory have established that students who are asked 'Why?' when they give an answer are more likely to remember their answer. Professor Daniel Willingham, in his article 'What will Improve a Student's Memory?' cites the illustration of students who were asked to remember that the western spotted skunk lives in a hole in sandy farmland, near crops. Students who were taught to ask themselves 'Why?' were more likely to recall the fact.

In time, if we keep asking them 'Why?', students will begin to realise that this is the key question to ask about anything they are learning. Once they begin asking 'Why?' for themselves, they have started thinking for themselves and so will have taken the essential step towards becoming an independent learner.

Pause and think

- Have I done my job well if my students have learned the right answers?
- What is missing when students say that all that matters is knowing what to write in a test?

6. The reality question

As well as 'Why?', the question 'What is it?' can serve as a good starter for getting students thinking, not least because as soon as we try to define things that we talk about all the time, we realise just how tricky the task is.

Ask your students to define a table. They will probably think of a dining table with four legs. But we use tables for all sorts of things – and they don't all have four legs. Some might not even have legs at all (try a quick Google Image search if you don't believe me).

If you now move on to some of the trickier concepts we use all the time when teaching, it becomes harder still to define them. 'What is it?' questions are great for getting students thinking more deeply about ideas they think they understand. If in the process they realise that often we can't give a definition, as these ideas have multiple meanings, they will have begun to appreciate something important about concepts. In the process they will hopefully become more curious and ready to question next time they come across a new idea, and it is questioning, as we've seen, that is the starting point for independent thinking and learning.

What is it? discussion starters

What is space?
What is meaning?
What is a number?
What is money?
What is a nation?
What is beauty?
What is truth?
What is music?
What is life?

What is justice?
What is the past?
What is a map?
What is a work of art?
What is beauty?
What is a nation?
What is a law?
What is an idea?

7. The value of values: exploring the ethical element of learning

We have seen that the hallmarks of flashpoint questions are that they are interesting, controversial and fertile. These are the types of question that bring discussion and debate to life in the classroom. Ethical questions are some of the best flashpoint questions of all. They are frequently questions that students care about and have their own views on, and by their very nature they tend to be controversial.

Moreover, when we begin thinking about values, we are led to the need for more facts. If we want to work out whether genetic engineering is ethical, we will need to find out what it is, how it works and what consequences it has. Ethical questions, then, make excellent starting points for classroom discussion and debate as well as for project work.

Once again, please don't make the mistake of thinking that these questions are limited to the humanities or arts. Everything that students learn raises ethical questions. Suppose you are teaching a chemistry class about the Haber process for manufacturing ammonia, a process that enabled mass-production of fertilisers, thus leading to the saving of many thousands of lives. But the very same scientist who did this work (Fritz Haber) also helped to develop the poison gas used horrifically in World War 1. Would it have been better for the world if he had never become a scientist? An ethical question like this is a starting point for research involving both scientific inquiry and personal reflection about questions of right and wrong.

Using ethical questions to stimulate thinking

- Whose fault is inequality?
- Should we allow human cloning?
- Do emerging economies have less responsibility to deal with climate change?
- How should we combat terrorism?
- Do we need more freedom of speech?
- Should we care more about animal welfare?
- Is it now unethical to use fossil fuels?
- Should there be positive discrimination in favour of minority groups?
- Should children have more say in the running of schools?

8. Semi-flipped programmes of study

I've been emphasising the value of classroom discussion as a starting point for getting students thinking. It also has a part to play once the learning process is underway. If you act as a Socratic mentor, stimulating the discussion by asking probing questions, the ensuing conversation can be a great way for students to consolidate their understanding and help each other iron out points of confusion.

This is particularly true if students come to the discussion having done some initial reading. I call this approach a 'semi-flipped programme of study'. Fully flipping the class means getting core information learned prior to coming to the lesson, and then using lesson time to focus on analysis and problem-solving. As I think there is a role for classroom instruction, I don't think we need to do a 'full-flip', but I do think that study prior to a classroom discussion is valuable. Here are some examples of how the technique works:

Student-led seminars

Ask students to read a short article and come ready to discuss it during a lesson. Invite one student to introduce the article. If you have a particularly confident student, they could also be asked to chair the discussion, allowing you the freedom to observe and monitor the level of understanding and thinking amongst the group. I find student-led seminars work best if the article is not too long or complex. It is worth having some basic comprehension questions prepared since these work well for getting the discussion started before going deeper into the issues.

Work-in-progress seminars

If students are working on projects, a work-in-progress seminar can be an effective way of helping them to clarify their thinking and receive beneficial feedback from their peers. Each student is invited to speak for two or three minutes about the research work they have been doing, then the rest of the class is invited to ask questions or make comments. These seminars are helpful because the act of trying to turn your research into a short presentation to an audience can really help the student to get a clearer understanding of what they are doing.

Student presentation

Invite one or two students to read their essay or make a presentation of the work they have done. You can then engage them in a Socratic conversation about their work, which can then open out to a whole class discussion. You will need a reasonably confident student for this to work and it is usually best to get them to submit their essays in advance so you can check that what they've written will be a productive starting point for the discussion. Incidentally, this is a very efficient way of combining teaching with verbal feedback!

9. Story-time

When asked to 'do some research' many students quite naturally begin by doing a Google search and, if they find suitable information, assembling this using a combination of cut and paste and (hopefully) some rewriting into their own words.

How can we get them beyond this stage? I find that it helps to ask students to organise their research so that their report tells a story.

I usually suggest that they plan to write up their research using a series of headings that cover the main aspects of the topic. If they decide early on what headings to use, they can slot new information into the sections of their report as they find it. This is much more efficient than making lengthy notes then trying to work out a way of arranging them.

Telling the story

The questions they should answer in their research include the following:

- What are the main historical developments in the topic they are exploring?
- Who are the main people that have been involved?
- What are the main arguments and ideas that have emerged?

If students can link their sources together, in either a chronological or thematic way, so that they form a coherent story, they will have taken a step beyond simple source selection and into the domain of analysis of sources.

10. Counter-arguing

A central theme of this book is that thinking begins when we are asked question to which more than one solution is possible. It is by puzzling over open questions that students begin to think for themselves.

Once they have thought of an answer that seems reasonable, one of the best questions students can ask themselves is: 'What is the strongest argument against my answer?'

We are all prone to various different kinds of cognitive bias and it is easy to jump to conclusions. Learning to counter-argue (to challenge your preferred viewpoint) is a vital step in learning to think more deeply and independently. Students who think for themselves do so by internalising the processes of discussion and debate. They learn to argue with themselves. This type of internalised, self-critical dialogue is at the very heart of independent learning in all subject areas.

Your role in all this is to act as the Socratic mentor. If you keep challenging your students to face up to counter-arguments and keep showing them that, when they do, they learn something new, they will eventually get the message and start acting as self-critical, self-reflective thinkers. Once you've got them to that stage, independent learning becomes something that happens naturally.

Encountering counter-arguments

It is not easy for students to identify or consider counter-arguments. Questions that can help your students include:

- Is there evidence that could be used against the argument you have just given?
- Why would someone disagree with the point you have just made?
- If you were going to argue against your own point of view, what would you say?

What to look for in a programme for developing independent learning

Up until now our focus has been on exploring what we mean by independent learning. We've defined it as teaching students to think for themselves. We've considered in broad terms how we can get students moving in this direction and looked at some specific techniques for helping students become more independent.

I've proposed a strategy that begins with thinking about the questions we ask, and finding ways to ask open-ended questions that act catalytically to provoke thought. From there, we help students to develop as thinkers by giving them space to engage in discussion and debate in the classroom. Further development happens through project work, which involves giving students some scope to choose what questions to explore and supporting them by Socratic mentoring as they engage in research and the development of their own ideas in response to their chosen question.

I am now going to suggest a number of different ways to incorporate versions of this strategy into your scheme of work.

The best of both worlds

When I talk to teachers about moving towards more independent ways of learning, they almost always say the same thing: 'I'd like to but there is so much stuff I have to get through. The curriculum is so full, how can I find time to fit in extra independent learning?'

I sympathise. We all know how important it is that our students get a good grounding in the things they need to know. But I've always felt that there is a false dichotomy here. It isn't a matter of throwing out the curriculum and embracing some sort of radically open-ended, unstructured, new approach, where the students alone dictate what they will learn. No, the point about independent learning is that it is an approach – a way of thinking about our teaching that aims to get students more actively questioning and thinking, and, as a result, understanding what they are doing better, and, finally, getting into a position where they know how to continue thinking and learning for themselves.

Over the years, I've experimented with various ways of threading this type of embedded independent learning into my schemes of work, allowing it to become the means through which the curriculum is explored deeply and engagingly, with the outcome that students learn core knowledge properly as well as having freedom to explore beyond the curriculum and think more deeply about what it all means.

The main point I want to make is that you don't need to throw away your existing schemes of work and start from scratch in order to get students thinking and learning more independently. The trick is to look at your scheme of work and spot the points where opportunities already exist to promote independence and make the most of these.

Here are some of the strategies I've used, or seen in action.

Learning-based projects

Project-based learning has its critics but something we can all agree on is that a learning-based project is worthwhile. What I mean by this is slotting in a small project (one to two weeks long) at the end of a unit as a way of allowing scope for students to explore more deeply and venture beyond the syllabus.

Putting a synoptic project into your scheme of work is a nice way of balancing the need to ensure the syllabus has been covered with the wish to encourage deeper learning and independent inquiry. A simple way of running a learning-based project is to give students a series of questions to choose from, with each question linked to some element of the topic they are studying.

With one of my Year Nine classes, having taught them some introductory material on space and the universe, I invited them to choose an exciting, open-ended question from a list of questions (e.g. What is a black hole? Are there parallel universes? What will happen to the sun?). Whilst these projects overlap with the syllabus to some extent, they were designed to go beyond it and allow space for real discovery of interesting ideas. So what about the syllabus? Well, we made sure we covered that with short, sharp bursts of instruction, backed up by rapid-fire tests. This way, we managed to include both instruction and independence in the unit.

Collaborative research for syllabus coverage

I find students appreciate revising using notes made as part of a group research exercise on Google docs. They produce them using a template that I share with them. The template has the syllabus headings for the topic and the co-workers then get to work researching to find information to slot in under the headings. This is another example of how we can get students working at tasks like research, either individually or in groups, so that they are working and learning independently, but still covering core syllabus material.

Review and think deeper

If you are anxious about getting through everything your students need to know, you might prefer to crack on with the syllabus, but try to squeeze in some time when a unit is done to engage in deeper, open-ended discussion and debate about the topic you've been teaching.

One nice example of this that I observed was a lesson taught by a colleague in the physics department of my school. At the end of the unit on astrophysics, he spent a lesson peppering the class with questions like 'Is there life elsewhere in the universe?' or 'Was the big bang the beginning?' This worked really well because the students had some knowledge of the topics that they could draw on, but also the questions took them into a realm where no one knows the answers – so there was plenty of scope for lively discussion and debate. In fact, as often happens, they started to protest that 'this is making my head hurt' – but they were enjoying the challenge, and definitely learning in a much deeper way than if they'd just spent the lesson ticking off the syllabus learning objectives.

One lesson, one problem

Sometimes we teach using a rapid-fire barrage of questions or problems, with worksheets giving plenty of opportunities for drilling students (and perhaps – dare I say it? – drilling them into the ground at times). You might well find that you can get students thinking better if you structure a whole lesson around a single question or problem. This gives time for them to experiment and explore different possible answers, ideally coming to a final answer as a result of thinking their way through the problem for themselves.

In one lesson with my Year Nine class, I simply set one task: 'Work out how fast the Earth is moving.' To do this they needed some data from me about how far from the Sun the Earth is, but the rest was up to them. What was nice about this activity was that because I allowed plenty of time for thinking, they worked out an answer by helping each other. One person suggested an equation. Someone else pointed out that it was missing something and another person supplied the correct formula. Normally I would have jumped in and told them how to work it out after a minute or two – but from the point of view of independent learning, it is better not to answer your own questions.

A puzzle like this can be approached using small groups, then snowballing to the whole class. The trick is to pick the right level: challenging but accessible. It is much more rewarding and confidence-building if students learn how to solve such problems for themselves.

Big question plenaries

In chapter four I proposed using open questions as catalysts to get students thinking. These work well as openers but also in plenaries. Having taught a topic, gather the class in a big circle around the front of the classroom (or around the edges) and spend a few minutes discussing an open-ended question with them. This should be linked in some way, if only tangentially, to the topic being studied. The benefit of working in this way is that you can give yourself time to 'cover what they need to know' whilst still factoring in time for deeper reflection and thinking. Opening up a big question for discussion at the end of a lesson is a great way of ensuring that they leave the lesson buzzing, thinking hard about what they've learned.

Peer instruction

Sometimes, we just have to tell students what they need to know. It would be a foolish defender of independent learning who opposed this basic fact. A certain amount of direct instruction is part of the process of developing independent learners. But there are ways of moving instruction beyond the traditional 'chalk and talk' format.

The American educator Eric Mazur made an important discovery about one such method. He found that when he was teaching physics to students, they struggled to grasp conceptual problems. Initially, he thought that all that would be needed would be to run an extra revision lecture for them. But it became clear that they still weren't getting it. More or less in desperation, he suggested that they take time during the lecture to talk to other students about the questions. This was the point when they began to understand. He realised what was happening: some students in the room had worked out what was going on with the conceptually challenging problems. Given time to discuss, they were better able to persuade others, partly because they understood the misconceptions, having only just worked their way to the right answer.

There are several features of Eric Mazur's method of using peer learning in the middle of directed instruction that are valuable. In the first place, it illustrates once again that we don't need to find ourselves choosing between 'traditional' teaching and 'progressive' inquiry or discussion-led approaches. We can mix both into our teaching.

Secondly, the value of the conversations that the students were having lay in the way that they helped students to address misconceptions. As we have seen, classroom discussion is most valuable in cases where there are alternative ways of thinking. Conversation happens most naturally and effectively when there are clear alternatives to explore, and in the case of Eric Mazur's students, allowing them time and space to explore these alternatives proved effective as a way of helping them progress towards a better understanding of the problems.

This methodology is emphasised by advocates of a constructivist approach to teaching, which emphasises the barrier to learning provided by the presence of misconceptions in the mind of the student. What Mazur's work suggests to us is that we can begin to address this difficulty by means of peer discussion, without having to overhaul an entire scheme of work. Of course, some might say that this isn't really independent learning – for the structure of the teaching and the choice of problems is directed by the teacher. But let's remember what we established in chapter one: at its heart, independent learning involves teaching students to think for themselves, and if students are working out answers through group discussion and debate, and coming to achieve better conceptual understanding, beyond what could have been provided for them by the teacher, I for one am happy to call that independent learning.

Pause and think

Watch Eric Mazur's video 'Memorization or understanding: are we teaching the right thing?' (https://www.youtube.com/watch?v=tn1DLFnbGOo).
Consider whether you could utilise peer instruction within any of your lessons.

Learn the scheme of work independently

I've been emphasising the opportunities to promote independent learning that exist within schemes of work. Sometimes, though, you might be in a position to start from scratch. Say you are beginning a new course and have to prepare a new scheme of work. How might you go about doing this in a way that will both cover the syllabus and encourage independence?

I once taught a philosophy course in which I was forever struggling to find a way to balance the need to cover the syllabus (of which there was a fair bit) with my wish – especially given the subject – to get my students engaged in the process of discussion and debate. I found that they could be quite resistant to exploring questions if they couldn't see a connection to the syllabus, and as a rule preferred me to 'tell them what they needed to know', whilst still enjoying the chance for some good argument from time to time.

In the end I found a way to satisfy both aims. I wrote a full scheme of work, which was linked to the syllabus content, with plenty of practice exam questions set as assignments, and a list of resources (book references, weblinks and podcasts that I recorded to provide an overview of the main syllabus topics). I gave the whole scheme of work to the students, who could then spend lessons and homework time working at their own pace through the assignments, with supervision from me. Effectively I was allowing them to work through the syllabus content as a sort of research exercise.

At regular intervals, we'd have a lesson in which we sat in a circle and I would introduce a topic for discussion, perhaps asking one of the class to read out their essay as a starting point (if I did this, I'd try to check the essay beforehand to make sure it sounded okay). This worked well as it allowed the student in question to get immediate verbal feedback from me (thus saving some marking time!) and from their peers. The discussion gave me a good idea of the level of understanding that the group had and it meant we could enjoy some open-ended argument whilst still feeling secure that we were covering the syllabus.

You'll probably recognise this as an example of the 'flipped classroom' (or semi-flipped classroom, as I called it in the last chapter, since some of the learning of content happened in the lessons). I was pleased to see that the group responded well to this approach. They were even happy to keep the discussions going more or less up until the exam, and their results suggested to me that they had acquired a good understanding of the syllabus material, whilst still having enjoyed a learning experience that incorporated discussion and debate and led to conversations that took us beyond the syllabus.

Chapter 5 takeaway

Teaching tip

Assess your students through project work

Since projects are processes that take place over a period of weeks, months or even a year or more, they tend to provide a context within which you can really get to know your students. Their strengths and weaknesses as learners become evident over time. Since you will be working as a facilitator, you will be able to observe, then provide appropriate guidance and form an in-depth assessment of how well they are learning.

Pass it on

Sharing ideas within your school

Create a display of project work for a school open day. Ask the students whose work is being exhibited to be ready to explain to the audience what they have done.

Colleague catch-up

Start conversations with colleagues about their experience with project work. What contexts have they used for introducing projects within their subject area? What opportunities for independent learning has project work provided? What challenges have they faced?

Share and tweet

Share ideas about the value of project work using the hashtag #BloomsCPD.

CPD book club recommendation

Peter Worley's book *The If Machine: Philosophical Enquiry in the Classroom* contains lots of good stimulus material for starting philosophical conversations with your students. (See Bibliography and further reading for details.)

Bloggers' corner

John Taylor 'From Monologue to Dialogue: Promoting Learning through Classroom Discussion' (https://www.cranleigh.org/our-school/academics/academic-enrichment/learning-and-teaching/blog/monologue-dialogue-promoting-learning-classroom-discussion/)

TO DO LIST:

☐ Think about the challenges of managing classroom discussion.
☐ Think about the challenges of project work.
☐ Consider the layout of the room in which you teach – is it conducive to discussion, debate and collaborative working?
☐ Try out some of the ten independent learning strategies in your classroom.
☐ Look for opportunities to engage students in project work.
☐ Read *The If Machine: Philosophical Enquiry in the Classroom*.
☐ Take a look at my blog 'From Monologue to Dialogue: Promoting Learning through Classroom Discussion'.

6

Assessing thinking in practice

We have been considering how to implement independent learning within our classrooms, both in general terms and at the level of specific techniques. There's one element we haven't explored: assessment. We'll begin, then, with a brief look at how we can assess the progress our students are making, and then we'll pause to evaluate our own progress with a second questionnaire, designed to help you reflect on the development of your understanding and practice since you began reading this book.

Informative formative assessment

I am going to suggest a few practical strategies for assessing thinking skills, but before I do, a word about the point of assessment. I'm sure you know of the important distinction between summative and formative assessment (and if you don't, you could consult Sarah Findlater's detailed and thoughtful guide to marking and assessment; see Bibliography and further reading). We tend as a rule to assess the products that emerge from the learning process: completed worksheets, handed-in essays and exam scripts. Yet we know that the feedback provided by marking is one of the most valuable tools for helping students move forward. Hence the value of formative assessment, which aims not simply to rank or grade students but to provide them with meaningful information about the current state of their knowledge and advice about what they should do next.

When it comes to the assessment of thinking skills, we should definitely focus on formative assessment. We have seen how important learning to think is, as a cornerstone for becoming an independent learner. We learnt to think by thinking, under the watchful eye of a teacher who can provide guidance on how well we're doing, and where and how we can improve. Formative assessment is thus a vital tool to have in our toolbags.

The title of this section refers to informative formative assessment. What I mean here is that we want to provide assessment feedback that can genuinely inform learning. I have in mind one of my own teachers, who used to scribble no more than one or two comments on each of my essays. Doubtless, I made many mistakes, but he knew how to put his finger on the ones that mattered – the points where a bit more thinking would help me take the next step.

How, in practice, can a formative model for assessment of thinking skills be applied? Here are a few suggestions:

Conversation tick sheet

At first glance it might seem ridiculous to try to assess something as subtle and complex as thinking skills using a tick sheet. But I find it can give a rough but still useful guide to how students are doing when they are participating in group discussion. One of the challenges in a group discussion is to keep track of who said what. A simple list with the names of students and a tick each time they contribute to the discussion will quickly show you which of the students are actively involved and which are more withdrawn. If you want more of a record of the students' responses, you can add brief comments (e.g. 'Made a good argument', 'Responded well to criticism'). This is a manageable level of assessment for a classroom exchange that may happen in quite a short space of time.

Climbing the logical ladder

In chapter five, we explored a model for discussion and essay writing that relied on the distinctions between point of view and argument, and argument and counter-argument. This model can help us when looking to assess the quality of students' thinking, whether this be in the context of a class discussion, an essay or a larger project.

There is a ladder of logic that runs from ideas to arguments, and from arguments to counter-arguments. Students get onto the ladder by making points, whether in a discussion or in a written response to a question. They show that they are moving up the ladder when they are able to support these points with evidence and argument. If they are able to go further, challenging arguments, giving counter-arguments or offering alternative interpretations, I would say they have moved to a still higher level. The ability to counter-argue – to identify an argument, and challenge it, offering an alternative set of reasons – is a hallmark of deeper thinking.

What does this look like in practice? The 'Logical Ladder' model is designed to help us assess how far our students have progressed, with higher positions corresponding to more sophisticated thinking. This is of course only one sort of assessment. It does not replace the assessment of work based on your expert knowledge of the topic students are studying. But it does provide a way of monitoring how things are going in terms of our goal of getting students thinking for themselves.

The first rung: ideas

Students can state arguments or make points clearly. They can identify what they think and express this. This stage is characterised by assertions such as 'What I think is...', 'My point of view is...' or 'I would say that...'

The second rung: reasons

Students can explain what makes them think the things they do. They can identify reasons for holding ideas and use evidence and argument to support them. You know your students are at the second rung when they start saying or writing things like 'I believe this because...', 'My reason is...' or 'The evidence shows that...', and their answers start using more sophisticated logical forms such as 'If... then...' sentences, or logical connectives such as 'therefore...' In general, they do not simply give answers or make points, but explain the reasoning behind these answers and the justification for the points.

The top rung: alternative interpretations

Students can identify and challenge arguments, giving alternative interpretations or showing how the evidence could lead to a different conclusion. We know when we are at this rung of the ladder when our students say things like, 'That argument doesn't work because...', 'That doesn't follow...', 'However...', 'But it could be argued that...', 'Alternatively...' or 'On the other hand...'

The ability to explore multiple different answers to a question is an indicator of mature, independent thinking. Have a look, next time you are reading a really good essay, at how frequently the student includes an alternative point of view or challenges an argument with a counter-argument. When a student is constantly looking to challenge a point with a counterpoint, you can be sure that student is thinking hard.

Criteria for essays

A simple model for assessing essays is to look for each of the elements in the logical ladder, and assess the sophistication of the thinking in the essay by how far up the ladder the student has climbed. An essay that is purely descriptive has probably required less thought than one that progresses beyond descriptive writing, into the analysis of arguments. An essay like this is, in turn, probably less sophisticated than one that involves argument and counter-argument, or the exploration and evaluation of alternative interpretations. Of course, this is not a hard and fast rule; a highly nuanced descriptive piece of writing will take more thought than a simplistic argument. But in general, I find that it takes more thought to progress beyond description into analysis and argument, and still more thought to explore the complexities of different interpretations.

A good example of using the Logical Ladder model to provide criteria for essays is provided by the 'Thinking Skills Assessments' that are now run by some universities as a selection tool. It is well worth looking these up online, as they provide a bank of good questions for getting students thinking, together with a marking grid that maps nicely onto the levels I've been describing.

By the way, please don't assume that the higher levels of the Logical Ladder are only accessible to bright students on their way to university. I find that students of all ages can engage in thinking at the higher level of interpretation and counter-argument; it is just that they tend to argue at age-appropriate levels, about topics that are accessible to them. The nice thing about the Logical Ladder from an assessment point of view is that you can apply it to questions of any level of complexity, ranging from whether dogs are better than cats to whether Einstein's philosophy of time was better than Isaac Newton's. In each case, the ladder suggests the next step a student can take. Have they formed some ideas? Then they need to give some reasons to support them. Have they formed some arguments? Then they need to challenge them by considering alternative interpretations.

Peer interview and peer feedback

I've said that we learn to think by thinking, and thinking that involves considering alternative possibilities and debating the merits of competing alternatives grows most naturally from dialogue. Now I must admit that if you catch me walking my dog across the Surrey Hills, you may well find that I'm engaged in some sort of dialogue with myself, trying out my latest ideas, then testing them by counter-arguing against them. It really helps to try your thoughts out loud. Better than a rather strange conversation with yourself, of course, is a dialogue with other people. This is where peer interview and peer feedback come in. Through these means, students can clarify their ideas and have them challenged in a setting where they feel secure. Peer feedback offers immediate and valuable formative assessment, which students may well be able to respond to more securely and confidently than they would if the comments came from their teacher.

I like to get students to engage in peer interviews at a stage when they are formulating their own ideas in response to material they have researched. The action of putting thoughts into words helps to focus and clarify them. I provide students with a set of questions for conducting the peer interviews, based on the Logical Ladder. What is their partner's point of view? What arguments would they give to support it? Have they identified alternative points of view and the arguments for them? How would they respond to these counter-arguments?

I often invite students to seek peer feedback at the end of a project too, when they are evaluating their progress. This is a nice way of encouraging them to be open to the comments and reflections of people other than their teacher. Let's not forget that once they are beyond formal education, they will be living with peer assessment throughout their working life.

Aristotle and the golden mean

Aristotle taught that the right path is often the middle way between extremes. Good advice for life, and good advice for assessment. On the one hand, there are those who are opposed to any form of assessment whatsoever; at the other extreme, and this is closer to where many of us find ourselves nowadays, every aspect of a student's work is measured in microscopic detail.

The right path is to assess but not to over-assess. As we've seen, students need us to give them our honest assessment of how well they are doing to help them do better and we can't ignore the fact that others will want to know how much they have learned, when formal education comes to an end and they seek to establish themselves in the wider world. But on the other hand, we can get obsessed with the desire to quantify everything a student does or says, in a manner that defeats the purpose of assessment, since the really useful formative assessment points get lost in the midst of a mass of data. Aristotle saw the right path when he commented that we should never look for more precision than the subject matter allows.

I mention this here because there are schemes that turn the assessment of thinking into a rigorous, formal system, with models of argument structure that spell out in detailed terms the particular logical forms that students are expected to know. This doesn't help. When we are assessing the quality of students' thinking, we need to make personal judgements. The element of judgement means that the process is going to be, to some extent, subjective. But this needn't be a problem, so long as we are aware of it and do all we can to be as fair and neutral as possible.

One way of achieving fairness is by treating our assessment judgements as part of an ongoing conversation. Suppose a student has failed to provide a good reason for their conclusion. Instead of simply stating this, if I put the point in the form of a question ('Can you explain more fully why you said that?'), I am helping the student take a step forward, rather than simply slapping on a label that says 'low-level analytical skills'. The more you can incorporate your assessment of thinking into an ongoing dialogue with your students, the better their progress will be. Our model for assessment of thinking is: first listen, then think, then ask and discuss.

Self-assessment

We've been looking at strategies for embedding independent learning within our teaching. Once up and running, we need to find out how things are going and then make decisions about what to change in order to move forwards. The questionnaire below is designed to help you reflect on ideas that you have tried out. This is a first step towards the topic we will be considering in chapter seven: a pedagogical audit. I use this phrase to refer to a process of examining aspects of teaching that relate to independent learning, asking specific questions as part of the lesson observation process, with a view to establishing targets (either individual or departmental) for moving ahead with independent learning.

How and why to complete the questionnaire

In order to keep progressing with your CPD it is vital that you reflect on your progress so far. Teachers may well be tempted to say at this point, 'But I know what I've done and what I'm strong and weak in.' However, without time spent in dedicated reflection, this is rarely the case. Quiet, focused time given over to real reflection brings to mind things that you might otherwise have neglected. It is thus time well spent. The important thing is to note down your reflections and findings and make a plan of action going forward as a result of your musings.

You will remember the questionnaire process from chapter two, but here is a reminder.

Quick response approach

If your preference for the self-evaluation is to go with your gut only, then simply fill in the quick response section after each question with the first thing that comes into your mind when you ask yourself the question. Do not mull over the question too carefully; simply read thoroughly and answer quickly. This approach will give you an overview of your current understanding and practice in using independent learning strategies. Just make sure you are uninterrupted, in a quiet place and able to complete the questionnaire, in one sitting, with no distractions, so that you get focused and honest answers.

Considered response approach

If you choose to take a more reflective and detailed approach, you can leave the quick response section blank and go straight on to reading the further guidance section under each question. This guidance provides prompt questions and ideas to get you thinking in detail about the question being answered and is designed to widen the scope of your answers. It will also enable you to look at your experience and bring examples into your answer to back up your statements. You may want to complete a few questions at a time and take breaks, or you may be prepared to sit and work through the questions all in one sitting to ensure you remain focused.

This approach does take longer, but it can lead to a more in-depth understanding of your current independent learning practice, and you will gain more from the process than the quick response alone.

Combined approach

A thorough approach would be to use both approaches together regardless of personal preference. There is clear value in both approaches being used together. This would involve you firstly answering the self-evaluation quick response questions by briefly noting down your instinctive answers for all questions. The next step would be to return to the start of the self-evaluation, read the further guidance and then answer the questions once more, slowly and in detail, forming more of a narrative around each question and pulling in examples from your own experience. Following this you would need to read over both responses and form a comprehensive and honest summary in your mind of your answers and a final view of where you feel you stand right now in your CPD.

This is the longest of the three approaches to this questionnaire but it will give you a comprehensive and full understanding of your current practice, thoughts and feelings in relation to using independent learning strategies in the classroom. You may be surprised at the difference you see between the quick response and the considered response answers to the same questions.

• I have done this self-assessment before. • I only want a surface-level overview of my current understanding and practice. • I work better when I work at speed. • I don't have much time.	**Quick**
• I have never done this self-assessment before. • I want a deeper understanding of my current understanding and practice. • I work better when I take my time and really think things over. • I have some time to do this self-assessment.	**Considered**
• I have never done this self-assessment before. • I have done this self-assessment before. • I want a comprehensive and full understanding of my current understanding and practice and want to compare that to what I thought before taking the self-assessment. • I have a decent amount of time to dedicate to completing this self-assessment.	**Combined**

Fig. 4 How should I approach the self-evaluation questionnaire?

Rate yourself

The final part of the self-evaluation is to rate yourself. This section will ask you to rate your attitude in each area that has been covered in the questionnaire with a view to continuing to work to improve in these areas. The table below shows how the scale works: the higher the number you allocate yourself, the more strongly you feel about your performance in that area.

Rating	Definition
1	Not at all. I don't. None at all. Not happy. Not confident at all.
2	Rarely. Barely. Very little. Very unconfident.
3	Not often at all. Not much. Quite unconfident.
4	Not particularly. Not really. Not a lot. Mildly unconfident.
5	Neutral. Unsure. Don't know. Indifferent.
6	Sometimes. At times. Moderately. A little bit. Mildly confident.
7	Quite often. A fair bit. Some. A little confident.
8	Most of the time. More often than not. Quite a lot. Quite confident.
9	The majority of the time. A lot. Very confident.
10	Completely. Very much so. A huge amount. Extremely happy. Extremely confident.

Fig. 5 Rate yourself definitions

Independent learning reflection questionnaire

QUESTION 1: What new things have you considered or tried that you have liked in terms of independent learning?

Quick response:

_____

_____

_____

_____

_____

Questions for consideration

- Are there any new areas of independent learning that you have tried in the classroom that you have enjoyed?
- Have you changed the way you approach lessons to incorporate more independent learning?
- How have your students reacted to changes you have made and new things you have tried? What did they like?

Considered response:

_____

_____

_____

_____

_____

Rate yourself

QUESTION 1: How happy are you that you have tried all you wanted to try in your approach to independent learning so far?

1   2   3   4   5   6   7   8   9   10

QUESTION 2: What changes have you made in your independent learning practice that you feel have had an impact upon student attainment and achievement in your classroom?

Quick response:

_____

_____

_____

_____

Questions for consideration

- Have you seen an impact on attainment and achievement as a result of any of the changes you have made or techniques you have implemented?
- When you have seen a positive impact, what had you done differently?
- Have you noticed whether students are more engaged with the new approach to independent learning?
- What have you tried that did not have a positive impact on student attainment and achievement? Would you try the same approach again but do it differently?
- Have you seen an impact on attainment and achievement for any particular group or age of student that perhaps you had not previously? Why is this?

Considered response:

_____

_____

_____

_____

_____

Rate yourself

QUESTION 2: How much impact on student achievement and attainment do you feel independent learning has made now that you have made changes to your practice?

| 1 | 2 | 3 | 4 | 5 | 6 | 7 | 8 | 9 | 10 |

QUESTION 3: How would you now describe your general approach to independent learning and how has it changed?

Quick response:

_____

_____

_____

_____

_____

_____

_____

Questions for consideration

- How has your everyday classroom practice changed?
- Do you mix up the independent learning approaches (discussion activities, research, project work) you use more than before?
- Are you now more confident about allowing students to make choices about the way they learn?

Considered response:

_____

_____

_____

_____

_____

_____

_____

Rate yourself

QUESTION 3: How happy are you with your approach to independent learning at the moment?

1	2	3	4	5	6	7	8	9	10

QUESTION 4: What parts of the educational research into independent learning interest you and how does this research inform and influence your practice?

Quick response:

_____

_____

_____

_____

_____

_____

Questions for consideration

- Do you feel more or less inclined to look into educational research concerning independent learning?
- Have you discussed any of this research with any colleagues?
- Have you conducted any research yourself, either individually or as part of a team within your school setting?
- How do you feel teachers or a school as a whole should use the findings of educational research into independent learning?

Considered response:

_____

_____

_____

_____

_____

_____

Rate yourself

QUESTION 4: How confident are you with your knowledge of educational research into independent learning?

1	2	3	4	5	6	7	8	9	10

QUESTION 5: What have you shared or discussed regarding independent learning with colleagues outside your department?

Quick response:

_____

_____

_____

_____

_____

_____

_____

Questions for consideration

- Have you shared any of your experience with independent learning with staff across the whole school?
- Have you sought discussions with staff in other departments or teaching years than your own?

Considered response:

_____

_____

_____

_____

_____

_____

_____

Rate yourself

QUESTION 5: How confident are you about sharing your ideas with others on a whole-school basis?

1   2   3   4   5   6   7   8   9   10

QUESTION 6: What have you shared or discussed regarding independent learning with colleagues in your department?

Quick response:

_____

_____

_____

_____

_____

Questions for consideration

- Have you shared your experience with independent learning with your department?
- Have you sought out discussions about independent learning with staff in your department?
- Have you worked with another member of your department on an independent learning project of any sort?
- Has anything changed in your department as a result of discussion or project work on independent learning?
- Have you influenced how independent learning is approached in your department through your discussions, suggestions or actions?

Considered response:

_____

_____

_____

_____

_____

Rate yourself

QUESTION 6: How confident are you about sharing your ideas with others on a departmental level?

1   2   3   4   5   6   7   8   9   10

QUESTION 7: Where do you feel your strengths now lie with respect to independent learning?

Quick response:

_____

_____

_____

_____

_____

_____

_____

Questions for consideration

- What would you now consider your strengths in terms of independent learning?
- Have these strengths changed since completing the last self-evaluation?
- Are there any elements of your approach to independent learning that you have been praised for by colleagues, students or parents?

Considered response:

_____

_____

_____

_____

_____

_____

_____

_____

Rate yourself

QUESTION 7: How confident are you about your strengths when approaching independent learning?

1	2	3	4	5	6	7	8	9	10

QUESTION 8: Where do you feel your weaknesses now lie when approaching independent learning?

Quick response:

_____

_____

_____

_____

_____

_____

_____

Questions for consideration

- What would you now consider are your areas for improvement in terms of independent learning?
- Have these areas changed since the last self-evaluation?

Considered response:

_____

_____

_____

_____

_____

_____

_____

Rate yourself

QUESTION 8: How much consideration do you give to any weaknesses in your approach to independent learning?

1	2	3	4	5	6	7	8	9	10

QUESTION 9: What approaches to independent learning would you like to try that you have not yet tried?

Quick response:

_____
_____
_____
_____
_____
_____
_____

Questions for consideration

- Since the last self-evaluation, have you spotted areas where you could include new techniques for independent learning?
- Are there techniques that you have read about in this book that you would like to try out?
- What is the next thing that you would like to try? How do you plan to go about it?

Considered response:

_____
_____
_____
_____
_____
_____

Rate yourself

QUESTION 9: How confident do you feel about expanding the range of techniques you use to enable independent learning?

| 1 | 2 | 3 | 4 | 5 | 6 | 7 | 8 | 9 | 10 |

QUESTION 10: Is there anything holding you back in developing your approach to independent learning?

Quick response:

_____

_____

_____

_____

_____

_____

_____

Questions for consideration

- Have you faced any challenges in developing independent learning? How did you address them?
- What training do you feel you are lacking with respect to the development of independent learning?

Considered response:

_____

_____

_____

_____

_____

_____

_____

Rate yourself

QUESTION 10: How much do you feel you are being held back in terms of developing your approach to independent learning?

1	2	3	4	5	6	7	8	9	10

QUESTION 11: Is there anything that you have tried as a result of reading this book so far?

Quick response:

_____

_____

_____

_____

_____

_____

_____

Questions for consideration

- Have you discussed the approach to independent learning described in this book with colleagues?
- Have you found any of the techniques described helpful in enabling students to begin to think for themselves?
- Have you involved the students themselves in the development of your approach to independent learning?

Considered response:

_____

_____

_____

_____

_____

_____

_____

Rate yourself

QUESTION 11: How confident do you feel about trying out new techniques for developing independent learning?

1   2   3   4   5   6   7   8   9   10

QUESTION 12: How have you involved your students in discussion of the impact of new approaches?

Quick response:

_____

_____

_____

_____

_____

_____

_____

Questions for consideration

- Have you carried out any questionnaire surveys with your students?
- Have you had any discussions with them about their attitude towards independent learning?
- How far have you moved in giving students some choice over the way in which they learn?

Considered response:

_____

_____

_____

_____

_____

_____

_____

Rate yourself

QUESTION 12: How confident are you about involving students in the process of developing independent learning?

| 1 | 2 | 3 | 4 | 5 | 6 | 7 | 8 | 9 | 10 |

The results

You've completed the questionnaire; now it is time to reflect on the ratings you have given yourself. The purpose of this second questionnaire is to help you reflect on the extent to which your approach towards independent learning has developed as a result of what you've been reading and put into practice in the classroom. Take a look at how you rated your answers for each question in this questionnaire and compare your ratings with the chart below.

Mostly low ratings

You still remain uncertain about the implementation of independent learning. That might be because you have not yet had time to begin to make changes, or perhaps you remain unsure about the way ahead. It would be worth reflecting on where your educational priorities lie. Do you see the need to move ahead with the task of creating more freedom for thought and inquiry in your classroom? Can you identify specific obstacles or challenges that may need to be addressed to make this possible? Is there an achievable first step you could take?

Mostly medium ratings

You have made a start with the exciting but challenging task of implementing independent learning in your classroom. You have perhaps begun to notice that this approach creates a different atmosphere in lessons, and that there is an impact on your students. There is still room for further progress, so it would be worth identifying areas that you feel need to be addressed next. It is also worth thinking about involving your colleagues. Are there teachers with whom you could discuss independent learning? Bear in mind that the end goal is to be in a position to help train others, as well as to have made progress yourself. Now would be a good time to start to explain to your colleagues that you have been exploring new approaches and are keen to involve them in the learning experience.

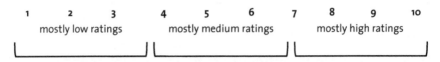

Fig. 6 How did you rate yourself?

Mostly high ratings

You feel confident about independent learning and have considered the impact of the approach you are using. You are in a good position to begin to think about how independent learning can be implemented more widely within your school. In the next chapter, we will consider the development of a school-wide strategy for independent learning and in part 2, we will address the creation of training programmes. Now would be a good time to begin conversations with colleagues about these matters. What are your school's priorities? Do others share your commitment to independent learning? Can you begin to identify areas for school-wide development? What training will be needed to make this possible?

Now what?

At one level, the journey you are on as you develop your approach to independent learning is a personal one; probably we will each have our own interpretation of what it means to give students freedom to think and learn for themselves. At another level, though, you are not on your own; it is likely that the questions you have been considering and the challenges you face are the same as those of your colleagues who share an interest in this area. The remaining sections of this book address the challenge of making the development of independent learning a school-wide venture. At the heart of this are the professional relationships between colleagues who share a sense that our approach to teaching and learning really matters; that this is something we should be working on individually and corporately.

It is important, therefore, that you foster the network of professional links that will enable each teacher to feel part of a group that is moving forwards together. This might or might not involve setting up formal meetings; it is just as likely that you will find support, and be able to offer it to others, through short chats over coffee or lunch. Keep in mind that these opportunities are valuable in helping to create and sustain a network of teachers who feel emboldened to experiment and innovate with their approach to their teaching.

Chapter 6 takeaway

Teaching tip

Keep in mind that independent learning and assessment happen through dialogue, not monologue.

Pass it on

If a colleague is unsure about how to assess a project or assignment that they have been supervising, ask them to sit with you whilst you provide verbal feedback to the student about the stage they have reached with their project.

Share and tweet

Share ideas that have emerged whilst doing the questionnaire on Twitter using the hashtag #BloomsCPD.

CPD book club recommendation

Wiliam and Black's *Inside the Black Box* (see Bibliography and further reading)

Bloggers' corner

Paul Langman 'How our college is cultivating independent learning in A level classes' (https://www.theguardian.com/teacher-network/2012/aug/23/independent-learners-a-level-classroom)

TO DO LIST:

- ❑ Keep your responses to the questionnaire in mind as you continue to teach.
- ❑ Look for opportunities to develop a network of teachers who are keen to explore independent learning in your school.
- ❑ Reflect on the way you assess the outcomes of independent learning.
- ❑ Check that there is a process for regular feedback to provide support whilst students are engaged in project work.
- ❑ Read *Inside the Black Box*.
- ❑ Read the blog 'How our college is cultivating independent learning in A level classes'.

7

Embedding and developing the practice

Drawing up a school-wide strategy for development

Is it possible for a school as a whole to move towards more independent learning? How can the practice of one teacher in one classroom form the starting point for the development of a school-wide strategy of promoting more thoughtful, reflective inquiry and self-directed learning?

There are challenges and obstacles facing schools that tend, on the whole, to discourage the movement towards giving students greater independence. We all know what these are: pressures of assessment and accountability lead towards a culture of 'teaching-to-the-test' and 'spoon-feeding', with students (plus parents, school administrators, governors, etc.) expecting that we teachers will 'tell them what they need to know' for their exams. Then there is the fact that modern syllabuses contain so much material and so much of it simply has to be learned. In these conditions, it can seem as though the default mode of standing in front of the class, telling the students what they need to know, then testing them on it, can seem the only way ahead.

But this isn't true. Each of us, within our own classroom, can adopt an approach in which students learn by thinking things through for themselves, with a greater emphasis on discussion, debate, inquiry and project work. And if it is possible for one teacher, it is possible for a school as a whole to move towards giving students greater independence.

To make this a reality, it is necessary for teachers to come to believe that things can change. The first step is to accept that change is possible and to do so by recognising that it actually happens. It may seem as though there are too many forces conspiring to prevent the way a whole school approaches teaching and learning from ever changing. But the argument that change is possible is a simple one, based on an observable fact: change happens. All it takes is for one teacher – and, given that you are the one reading this book, my guess is that this one teacher is likely to be you – to change the way they teach, using the sort of techniques described in this book to refute the assertion that change is impossible. All that is required, if independent learning is to diffuse itself throughout a school, is for this pattern to be taken up and adopted by others.

The mechanism for this is as follows. Exemplification comes first. For other teachers to make a change, they need to see independent learning in action, in order to show convincingly that it can be done, and to stimulate ideas about how they could do it themselves.

Following exemplification comes the creation of a culture of support for independent learning. It takes time, determination, resources and patience for a change like this to happen and become embedded within a school's educational culture. This support will take the form of professional development conversations, training opportunities, lesson observations and feedback. A central component of the support programme is what I term 'pedagogical audit', a process in which a teacher or department identifies aspects of their practice that they would like to change – in our case, related to independent learning – then goes through a process of lesson observation, professional dialogue, reporting and reviewing, with a view to allowing the nature of the development process to emerge naturally, in a manner that is adapted to their circumstances. We will look more closely in this chapter at how pedagogical auditing can be implemented on a school-wide basis.

Having exemplified change and begun to create a culture of support to enable it to be embedded, the third stage is to articulate and promote the principles underpinning the change on a school-wide basis. This will involve drawing up a philosophy of change, highlighting it through staff CPD sessions and other high-profile events, such as dedicated teaching days during the year, when everyone is expected to try it for themselves, and explaining and promoting the approach to stakeholders, including students, parents and school governors.

The final stage is to establish means of assessing the impact of the new approach and carry out a systematic evaluation of its effectiveness, with a view to learning lessons about how it can be modified in future iterations.

Pause and think

How would you describe the culture of learning in your school? What are the points where change will be needed if there is to be more independent learning? Who would you say would be most willing to embrace a new approach?

Change from ground level up

I want to emphasise that this is very much a ground-level-up model to creating a school-wide culture of independent learning. In my experience, and I think this is true of much effective innovation in the educational world, change happens when groups of committed teachers share a new vision of what could be done then work together to support each other in widening the sphere of influence to include those who may initially be cautious about embracing change, or even outright reluctant.

It is important to be realistic and sympathetic about the challenge of doing things differently. Frankly, teaching is hard work at the best of times and changing the way we teach adds an extra layer of challenge, complexity and demand. It won't work unless teachers know that they will be supported and that they are not being asked to do something that seems completely impossible.

This is the reason why, when I am working with colleagues, I am constantly looking for overlap between the conception of independent learning that I wish to encourage and elements that I can see within their existing practice. One of my mantras is: 'independent learning is just good teaching'. In this way, I am trying to portray the shift towards more independent learning as a change of emphasis, or focus, rather than a revolution in the classroom that would require throwing away much that already exists and is of value. We will have to wait a very long time indeed for any such revolution, and I'm not convinced that, once the costs have been weighed against the benefits, the net effect would justify it.

This is particularly true if the change has been imposed from above. Top-down is less likely to succeed than bottom-up. The adoption of a more independent approach to learning and teaching begins within the heart and mind of the teacher, and winning hearts and minds is both the first and most essential step towards change. A programme for creating more independent learning within a school will fail if it does not begin by bringing teachers on board with the vision. The path to change is evolutionary, not revolutionary. Once colleagues appreciate this, they will feel reassured and many of the barriers to change will fall away.

Beginning at the beginning

The cornerstones of the model of independent learning that I have been advocating are Socratic dialogue, in which students discuss open-ended questions under the guidance of a Socratic mentor, and project work, in which they pursue meaningful, deep, challenging questions through processes of research, inquiry, argument and counter-argument.

I've suggested that these elements of independent learning can be woven into the curriculum in more or less any subject area. However, it must be said that it is a challenge to develop dialogue and project-based learning within a context where there is a fixed curriculum that specifies that particular subjects need to be studied. These may or may not work well as starting points for discussion and inquiry. At the very least, some work needs to be done to establish where best to insert independent learning within the curriculum (finding these points is one of the main objectives of the pedagogical audit process).

I therefore advise that the best way to start getting independent learning going on a school-wide basis is to create space within the timetable for a customised programme, dedicated to using the techniques described in the earlier chapters of this book. There are qualifications such as the Extended Project, IB Theory of Knowledge and Extended Essay and the Pre-U Global Perspectives, as well as opportunities for non-assessed programmes that can be taught as part of citizenship, PSHE or curriculum enrichment programmes. The great merit of using contexts like these is that they provide excellent training grounds for teachers who want to explore what it means to facilitate dialogue or mentor student researchers, without the added complication of having at the same time to teach their way through a set of assessed syllabus topics.

This sort of enrichment of learning should happen within the timetable, as part of day-to-day teaching. But space is tight, and if you are not in a position to find lesson time, a great deal of good work can happen in extra-curricular settings, through a club or society, or as part of weekly tutor group meetings. All you need is a period of time – even a few minutes a week during lunchtime, if that is all that is available – when you can get a group of students together to function as a 'community of inquiry', discussing ideas in a free setting, where it is expected that the students will take the lead and everyone's ideas will be taken as seriously as everyone else's.

If you have the opportunity to use these discussions as a launch pad for project work, so much the better. If time is really tight, the project work can happen outside school hours, with occasional meetings for support. Ideally, though, some timetabled time should be provided for students to receive regular, systematic support and guidance, such is the importance of project work as a vehicle for the development of students' independence.

Pause and think

Where could you find curriculum space for project work? Is there a place within the timetable where independent learning could be developed? Are there co-curricular contexts where it is happening already, and could happen more?

The principles of pedagogical audit

As I've indicated, pedagogical audit is designed to provide a way of widening the sphere within which we encourage students to learn independently, until it covers the whole curriculum. Here is how the process works:

1. **Agree on aims**. The audit process is designed to help a department move forwards in a particular direction. This direction needs to be defined clearly from the start, as it will provide the criteria by which to assess current practice and determine targets for development. Examples of the aims that might be set include promoting discussion and debate within the classroom, encouraging independent research, asking challenging questions to get students thinking, giving meaningful feedback to students or incorporating more project work into programmes of study. It is best to keep the focus of an audit cycle simple and specific. Choose one or two key areas so that there is not too much being asked of everyone.

2. **Audit begins with listening**. In fact, the word derives from the Latin word 'auditus' meaning 'hearing'. The decision to set the direction of a pedagogical audit process should involve discussion and consultation. People need to agree on the focus for the process. Once the focus has been agreed, the next step is to gain a sense of what is happening in the classroom through lesson observation. We'll come back to this in a moment, but a crucial point is that these lesson observations are not intended to provide a mark, grade or assessment but instead should suggest areas that can form the basis of professional conversations about development. It cannot be stressed too highly that observation alone will achieve little or nothing. Development happens when, through dialogue and discussion, agreement emerges about areas for change.

3. **Audit is a cycle**. Once you have chosen a focus, observed, discussed, provided feedback and agreed upon targets for development, after a suitable interval, another cycle can begin, the focus of which is to see the extent to which the agreed-upon targets have been met, together with the establishment of new targets.

4. **Each stage of audit needs explanation**. I usually conduct audits one department at a time. I begin by meeting with the department, briefing them on the nature of the process, sharing with them the agreed-upon focal areas for the observations and explaining how the ensuing report will be shared. Once the process is underway, I liaise with the Head of Department about other aspects, such as work scrutiny, that can feed into the evidence base for the report. Finally, once the report is written, I share it with the Head of Department, then the Department, and finally, with the Academic Leadership Team in the school. I might also share brief findings with other colleagues if that seems helpful as part of the drive towards a school-wide approach to independent learning.

Using lesson observation to help embed independent learning

Lesson observation: handle with care

Lesson observation is a valuable element within the audit process, but it needs to be approached in the right way. The first point to note is that it is not to be used to hold teachers to account. The point of observations happening within a pedagogical audit cycle is to gather information and form a picture of practice. It is worth remembering that the research on lesson observation highlights that individual observations, even when made by trained observers, do not provide a reliable picture of a teacher's abilities. There are so many variables that go into determining whether or not learning is happening, and as we saw when we considered the research, one of the crucial ones (namely, the extent to which students are thinking about what they are learning) is not easily measured, and certainly can't be measured from a single-lesson snapshot.

We must treat observation as a single source of information, and use it, in conjunction with professional conversations, work scrutiny and other evidence-gathering (not least, from the teacher's own self-assessment of their practice), to form an overall picture. Even then, we need to bear in mind that if we did the same exercise under different conditions (at a different time of year, for example, or with different classes), we might see a quite different picture.

For these reasons, I am very cautious indeed about drawing inferences from lesson observations. They work best simply as starting points for a discussion, the purpose of which is to explore what the teacher understands by things like 'independent learning', whether they can see elements of it in their own practice, and whether they can identify ways it could be developed further.

Stay focused

I expect you have seen lesson observation forms that try to cover everything: differentiation, use of IT, assessment and so on. The point of observations that happen as part of a pedagogical audit is, however, more restricted. The audit cycle should address one or two focal areas and the lesson observations should address specific elements within the lesson. For this reason, I prefer not to use a lesson observation record sheet with lots of boxes to fill. I keep it simple: a form with space for notes about the lesson, plus reminders at the top about the areas being audited (e.g. 'independent learning').

When I'm observing, I make notes on activities that relate to the focal area. So, for example, if a teacher runs a discussion activity, I will make notes on the arrangement of the class at the time (were the chairs arranged in a manner that facilitated discussion?), the style of questioning that was used, the way in which the teacher facilitated the dialogue (e.g. with use of question-bouncing), the amount of time spent on the activity, and its relationship to other elements in the lesson.

I like to record some of the best quotes from the lesson, either questions or statements from the teacher, or short snippets of dialogue that illustrate the kind of interchanges going on. These can be used to fill out the picture painted in the final report.

It's the thought that counts

One element that any lesson observer will want to consider is student activity: what are the students actually *doing* during the lesson? With our emphasis on learning through thinking, we can be more specific. We will want above all to observe the extent and quality of the thinking that is going on in the lesson.

Pause and think

At various points throughout this book I've referred to Professor Robert Coe's admirable dictum: 'Learning happens when people have to think hard.' With this in mind, crucial questions to consider include these:

- What are the points in the lesson when students are being made to think?
- Were questions asked that prompted thought?
- Were there opportunities for thinking to develop through discussion?
- Were the best activities from a thinking point of view confined to the start or end of the lesson?

This last bullet point is significant as I think that it is not uncommon for teachers to include a good, thought-provoking activity during a starter or plenary, but for time for these activities to be curtailed. Just when the discussion starts to get interesting and the ideas begin to flow from the students, you can tell the teacher begins to feel more pressure to 'move on' and 'get to the things they need to know'. At times like these, it is worth asking: could I plan to allow more space and time for discussion? If you feel you haven't got time to allow the discussion to run on, it might mean saying to the class: 'These are great ideas; hold onto them, and we'll return to the discussion' then planning to give a future lesson over to discussion and debate.

Feedback through professional conversations

I am always conscious that any lesson I teach could have been improved in numerous ways. If someone was observing me, I'd like to discuss with them on a professional basis, explaining the reasons why I did what I did and giving my own assessment of how and why it worked. If they have helpful suggestions, I'd be happy to feed them into my own ongoing thinking about my professional practice.

I'm sure we all work in much the same way. The habit of self-reflective evaluation is an instinct that we develop as a result of the need to learn from experience, which is essential as teaching is not a theoretical activity but an intensely practical one.

It is worth keeping these points in mind when giving feedback to colleagues. I always try to frame my comments as questions. 'Would it have been worth giving more time for discussion?' 'There was an excellent discussion that began in the last few minutes of the lesson – could the lesson be revised so that this happened earlier on?' 'Some of the children were seated with their backs to others – could you rearrange seats so that everyone has eye contact with everyone else?' And so on. In framing my feedback in this way, I'm aiming to be a Socratic mentor – to exemplify the habit of stimulating thought and learning through questioning. The great advantage of putting things this way, rather than by issuing instructions, is that the comments can then form the basis for an ongoing professional dialogue. It shows respect for the teacher's judgement and awareness of the necessarily limited context of the single period lesson observation. For all I know, the teacher's answer to my questions might be: 'Yes, we did just what you suggested last week, which is why I was doing it differently in this lesson.' Questions that stimulate reflection and discussion are the order of the day, not precipitous judgements.

Pause and think

When you have received feedback, what have you found useful, and less useful, about how it was provided? How do you approach giving feedback to colleagues? Would you describe yourself as a directive leader or a collaborative colleague?

The final report: highlight achievement, signpost ways forward

To bring the audit cycle to completion, I gather together short summaries of my lesson observations and write an overview of the progress that I've seen in relation to the agreed-upon focus for the audit. The key point to the report is that I'm looking to show that the move towards greater independence starts with things most of us are already doing. We ask questions designed to get students thinking, we use elements of discussion in one way or another and we usually make use of projects. What I do in reporting is to highlight these elements of good practice then ask questions about how they could be developed.

The point of framing a report in this way is connected to a central theme of this book. If you see independent learning as a radically new paradigm for education, which requires us to tear up everything we've been doing and start afresh, you might as well kiss goodbye to any hope of seeing more of it happening in the classroom. There won't be a revolution anytime soon – we're all just too busy, I'm afraid, even if there was a compelling case for wholesale transformation. But the point I've been keen to emphasise is that we can move forwards not by a staging a classroom revolution but by slow and steady evolution. We just need to identify the parts of our lessons that work well for getting students thinking for themselves and then ask how we can create more of them. The merit of putting any recommendations arising from your audit in this form is that you stand a decent chance that your colleagues will be prepared to listen and give them a try.

Keep the wheel rolling

A nice feature of the audit process is that it is iterative. Once a report has been written and some areas for development have been highlighted, there should be an opportunity in the future to revisit them. I'm currently trying to work my way around the different academic departments in my school, typically seeing two or three per term. At this rate, a school-wide audit will take about three years. The plan is that after the first cycle is complete, I'll be revisiting, reminding colleagues of the points we established as priorities during the first cycle, and looking to see whether things have progressed. This leaves open various possibilities. We might agree that targets were met, or that more needs to be done, or perhaps the targets weren't met and might in fact not have been appropriate, and thus need revision.

The emphasis throughout is that audit is a process that is jointly owned. We all have a say in what we think needs to be done to achieve our goal of getting students to think and learn more independently.

Chapter 7 takeaway

Teaching tip
The quality of your professional relationships is the foundation on which the success of your efforts to develop school-wide independence depends.

Pass it on
Write brief summaries of some of the best moments in lessons you have observed for your Teaching and Learning noticeboard.

Share and tweet
Share ideas about the value of pedagogical audit using the hashtag #BloomsCPD.

CPD book club recommendation
I discuss ideas for developing independent learning on a whole-school basis in my book *Think Again: A Philosophical Approach to Teaching* (see Bibliography and further reading).

Bloggers' corner
Read Eddie Playfair's blog 'Promoting a sixth form student research culture' (https://eddieplayfair.com/2014/09/02/promoting-a-sixth-form-student-research-culture/)

TO DO LIST:

- ❏ Consider where there is scope to develop project work either within or alongside your curriculum.
- ❏ Discuss the development of a pedagogical audit programme with colleagues.
- ❏ Agree on the aims of an audit programme.
- ❏ Plan a timetable for departmental lesson observations and feedback sessions.
- ❏ Highlight good practice in independent learning.
- ❏ Read about steps that can be taken to change the culture of a school in order to promote genuinely independent learning in *Think Again: A Philosophical Approach to Teaching*.
- ❏ Read Eddie Playfair's blog 'Promoting a sixth form student research culture'.

Part 2

Train others

1 Planning and preparing CPD

It is time to move onto the question of what your school CPD for independent learning will look like. The aim of part 2 of this book is to help you plan, prepare and deliver training programmes that will equip colleagues in your school to begin implementing the approach to independent learning outlined in part 1.

Now if you have been involved in doing any training of teachers, you will know that it is a valuable, indeed vital, role, but a potentially delicate and challenging one. Bluntly, we teachers prefer to be up there teaching; we're not always the best at being taught. We tend to sit through CPD sessions, recognising in theory how important they are, but tending in practice, unless we have a specific need or interest, to have one eye on the clock. If I've got lessons to prepare and books to mark for tomorrow, thinking through the basis of my approach to teaching is not going to be top of my agenda and given how busy we are throughout the year, this will be true more or less at any time you schedule a CPD slot. There's also an issue of authority. If you are the one who is stepping up to the podium to speak to your colleagues, they will be wondering what you know that they don't.

We'll see that there are ways of pitching training to address these challenges, but it is important to be aware of them from the outset. Here, in quick-fire succession, are a few of the objections or challenges you might confront when you start to set up or run your CPD programme. I've included rapid rebuttals. I won't go into more detail as most of this ground has been covered in part 1. Think of this as a prompt sheet to check before you announce your programme.

Challenges for trainers

SLT buy-in

Comment (from a distracted senior leader in your school): 'It sounds good – happy to let you get on with it by yourself.'

Response: 'I am proposing that the development of independent learning across the whole school should be one of our CPD priorities. If teachers are to get behind this, it will need endorsement and support from the SLT so that it is taken seriously by everyone.'

The time factor

Comment (from a bleary-eyed colleague): 'It sounds good but I just don't have time to fit anything else in – there's already so much stuff I have to cover.'

Response: 'Independent learning is like a chemical catalyst. A little drop added in can really energise things. You won't need to teach lots of extra content. It's about an approach that encourages students to think more for themselves.'

Misunderstandings of independence

Comment (from a sceptical teacher): 'Are you saying we should expect students to teach themselves? I can't see that working very well with the bottom set.'

Response: 'Independent learning means teaching students the skills they need to think for themselves. It isn't a matter of leaving them on their own and hoping they'll work it out by themselves – they'll still need our support.'

Independent learning versus direct instruction

Comment (from a serious teacher-blogger): 'Research shows that direct instruction works best. We should just tell them.'

Response: 'Research shows that direct instruction and independent learning both have a place. We begin by instructing students but expect them to become more independent as their knowledge and skills grow.'

Reluctance to change

Comment (from a jaded colleague nearing retirement): 'We tried this before, you know, and it didn't work.'

Response: 'The world is changing and it's important that we prepare our students for a future where they'll be expected to think for themselves and continue learning new things. It's worth giving it a try – students often respond really well to a new approach.'

Worries about exam results

Comment (from a concerned academic deputy head): 'At the end of the day it's the results that matter, you know.'

Response: 'No one is suggesting we give up on exams. If we teach students to think for themselves, not only will they be prepared for life beyond school, but they'll be able to show more depth of thought in their exam answers too.'

Student buy-in when a school is not used to independent learning

Comment (from a confused student): 'Can't you just tell us what we need to know?'

Response: 'Universities and employers tell us that they want students who know how to think for themselves. Don't forget as well that sometimes we just don't know the right answers and all of us have to think for ourselves.'

What training is needed

Comment (from a curious colleague): 'We've not had any training on this. How do we start?'

Response: 'I'm glad you asked! We're planning a programme with lots in it to help you...'

Moving forwards

What contexts work best?

When does CPD happen? There are identifiable sessions a few times a year, and perhaps ongoing programmes on a more regular basis. We'll be looking shortly at plans for sessions like this. But if I reflect on my own experience, I am quite sure that much of the most effective CPD I've experienced has happened in other contexts.

My paradigm for CPD is just like my paradigm for learning: it happens through dialogue, not monologue, and it happens through interactions between Socratic mentors and those who need some supervisory guidance – a nudge, a tip, a suggestion, a hint, a question – something that makes them think, and realise what they could be doing differently and better. In other words, we learn best when we are on the job, reflecting on what we are doing and talking about it with other colleagues, who may be more experienced, or more expert, or simply willing to listen thoughtfully and ask questions until we begin to see things differently ourselves. Thus, CPD needs to be seen as something ongoing that happens through professional conversations.

Micro and mini CPD

It is easy to think that there simply isn't enough time for all the CPD that needs to be done. But we think that because we think CPD happens only through formal training sessions, at the start of term or on the occasional day away from school for a course. In fact, much of the most effective CPD happens informally, through brief exchanges in the staffroom, or ideas shared during a departmental meeting or conversations following an observed lesson. Peek into the gaps in between other activities and you'll find plenty of CPD-rich interactions going on.

I call these short, informal, practical conversations 'micro CPD' and 'mini CPD'. An example of micro CPD would be a quick chat with a colleague along the lines of 'How would you teach topic X to Year Y?' or 'Can you show me how to set up a Kahoots quiz?' A mini-CPD session would be a 15-minute activity within a departmental meeting exploring how to create scaffolded project assignments on Google classroom.

I strongly recommend that you utilise micro and mini CPD as much as you can. Partly this is because it is true that there would never be enough time, if we were relying on formal sessions, but also I think we teachers tend to be more receptive to ideas if they are shared in relaxed, informal conversations. This way, we neatly skirt around the obstacle of the slight resentment that can arise when teachers are expected to listen to a colleague who is seen to be setting themselves up as 'an expert'. With CPD for independent learning, as with independent learning itself, it is better to be a guide at the side.

Co-teaching arrangements

I've suggested that when it comes to CPD it is best to see our relationship with our colleagues as one of co-development of skills and knowledge. A nice way of exemplifying this is by co-teaching arrangements. One teacher who has greater knowledge of certain techniques (say, project-based learning, or management of classroom discussion, or use of IT for research purposes) can take the lead, guiding the class with active support from a colleague who may be new to this way of working.

I find that this arrangement works well. At one level, the more experienced teacher is guiding the class, but at another level, they are exemplifying how to teach the technique to their colleague. Seeing a technique being put to work is far better than reading about it or even discussing it. It quickly becomes obvious how it works and, likely as not, some of the common problems will crop up and there'll be a chance to see what contingency plans are necessary ('Your laptop battery's dead you say? There's a free desktop in the corner of the room').

If it is a matter of managing a discussion seminar, one teacher can take the lead, with the other contributing, or they can agree to split the class and each take a smaller group, with the more experienced teacher providing oversight.

One of the biggest barriers to progress with independent learning is teacher confidence and one of the best ways of building this is to invite a colleague to join a lesson where they will discover that there's nothing magical or mysterious about independent learning. It is mainly a matter of doing more of the things that most of us do some of anyway, like asking more open-ended questions and giving students more time and freedom to respond.

Shared development of programmes of study

Suppose you want to help a department incorporate elements of independent learning into one of their programmes of study. Sharing in the process of writing a scheme of work is one way of helping them see what is possible. Bearing in mind that the best way of developing independent learning across the whole school is not to ask colleagues to start afresh, the strategy of developing elements in a scheme of work where there is space for discussion, debate, individual research, project work and presentations is the way to go.

Another strategy for co-developing a scheme of work is to set up a shared Google doc with links to different topics, and invite colleagues to share in the creation of sections of the scheme, following a model you have developed. For example, for the taught component of an extended project programme, I have written a sequence of lessons designed to encourage students to engage in discussion and debate, in order to develop their reasoning skills before they get into project work, and to suggest interesting topics that they might like to investigate when they choose their project titles. I write a few of these using some of the discussion techniques we've looked at, such as Socratic seminars, think, pair, share exercises, student-led seminars and class debates. The teaching team then discuss what topics we'd like to include and different teachers contribute lesson plans to address topics of which they have expert knowledge. This way, we share expertise, and jointly develop a programme through which is threaded the pedagogical elements that underpin independent learning.

Training others by modelling independence in your own teaching

As well as co-teaching and sharing in the development of programmes of study, you can share ideas about independent learning by modelling them in your own teaching, with colleagues invited to join to observe lessons. Over the years, I've often been asked by teachers to explain how I run project-based learning and I usually suggest that the teacher joins one of the sessions to see how it works in practice. This is an ideal arrangement. I can continue to work with the group, managing discussions, providing mentoring support, offering advice and so on, and the observer can see what sorts of project the students are working on, and learn through discussion with them and with me what the challenges are, and what has helped the students to make progress.

If I use this arrangement for observation, I try to take time during the lesson to explain to the observer what is happening and how the classroom activity relates to the overall process of project work. I also try to find time for follow-up discussion afterwards, perhaps over lunch. The great advantage of this way of modelling and demonstrating techniques is that independent learning is demystified: it becomes clear what it means in practice to have students engaging in independent research projects, for example, and there is a real sense of the penny dropping as the teacher who is observing comes to appreciate how they could do it too. It is much, much easier to explain independent learning to a colleague who has seen it in action in a setting like this.

Using independent learning within the training process itself

When you are running a formal training session, it is worth ensuring that some of the training activities you use are chosen to give colleagues an opportunity to learn independently. This happens when you allow time and space for questioning, discussion and exploration. Sometimes this happens because a question-and-answer session is scheduled into the programme, or time is allocated for group discussion, when they are invited to share ideas about the development of a scheme of work, for example. But as I've mentioned, some of the most effective micro-CPD interactions happen informally, when teachers ask the questions they are most concerned about over coffee, or during a quiet chat whilst other teachers are arriving for the session. Make sure you allow time for this sort of discussion and don't make the mistake of rushing through such conversations in order to 'get on with the training'. Often, it is these discussions that are the training.

Drawing up a development plan for school-wide independent learning

As you look to involve more colleagues from your school in the move towards independent learning, a development plan will be needed. The purpose of this document is to enable planning of activities so that the different elements of the initiative are coordinated, properly staffed and well-resourced, backed by appropriate professional development opportunities and also subject to evaluation. I would preface the action plan with a statement about the nature of independent learning and a list of the various planned activities. An extract from a plan, loosely based on one I wrote for my school, is here:

The development of independent learning

What we mean by independent learning

- Teaching students to think for themselves by participation in discussion and debate in lessons and through project work.

We are committed to independent learning because

- We believe this is important for students' personal development as autonomous learners and creative individuals.
- We believe that learning is deeper and richer when students are actively involved in making choices about the learning process.

How we will embed independent learning

- The appointment of a Director of Independent Learning.
- Creation of a programme for project-based learning.
- Expansion of opportunities for discussion and debate in the classroom.

Action plan for the coming year

Action	Timescale	Staffing requirements	Resource requirements	CPD	Monitoring and evaluation
Implementation of a programme for project-based learning	June 2017 – June 2018	3 staff to supervise taught course and provide student mentoring, 3 periods per week	Staff time allocation Online research sources IT rooms MOOCs* offering guidance on the project process In-school VLE with student guidance	Information about programme during whole staff CPD Teaching team CPD day during summer term 2017 Mentor training Sept 2017	Student feedback surveys addressing attitudes towards learning Staff survey addressing confidence to use independent learning

*MOOCs: massive open online courses

In drawing up the plan, it is worth thinking about what is realistic, given the staff time you have available. For example, suppose you want to introduce project work at different ages. It makes sense to begin with one year group, get that programme running, then move to begin work with a different year group. For example, you could set up a project programme for Year Twelve one year, let it run for a second so you can evaluate its impact, then begin a project programme for Year Ten students. In terms of demands on staff time, there are obvious benefits, and you can also plan to provide appropriate professional development for your core team who will be part of the first wave of implementation, with extra support provided for those who will join later. Probably some of the staff who are involved in the first wave can assist with the second, taking on the role of co-teachers or 'expert mentors' who can help colleagues who are coming new to project supervision.

The other thing that a development plan enables you to do is to look at what can be done to promote more independent learning and thinking in all areas of school life. For example, could group discussion activities be developed further within PSHE? Could tutor sessions include some student-led discussion of ethical questions? Could the teaching of research skills be embedded in an IT programme?

This leads us naturally on to consider opportunities for embedding independent learning across the curriculum.

Locating curriculum openings

The process of professional development involves working with colleagues to identify points within the curriculum where independent learning can occur. Not all topics lend themselves to dialogue and debate, or project work, and so the best thing is to look for promising openings and build on these. Often, for example, some project work will already feature within a scheme of work, and it may simply be a matter of developing this further. For example, suppose you have been teaching students to use open-access journals through search engines such as www.opendoar.org during their project lessons. You can then do some mini CPD with other departments to show them how this tool could be useful when they are doing projects or research assignments.

It might be also worth using a slot in a whole-school CPD session, if you have the opportunity, to brief colleagues on the tools that are available and that students have been trained to use. Alternatively, you could highlight techniques for independent learning during a pedagogical audit of a department, demonstrating some of these as part of the review meeting at the end of the audit, with a recommendation that they be embedded in schemes of work.

Identifying and supporting champions

If you stand up in the staffroom or at a school CPD session and explain that the school is aiming to promote independent learning, you can be fairly sure that there will be a spectrum of responses, ranging from enthusiastic support, through to curiosity, scepticism and outright opposition. As we saw in chapter one, the phrase 'independent learning' has multiple interpretations and a sceptical reaction to some of these is entirely appropriate. We've considered what you need to do in order to start winning colleagues over. The main advice I'd give is to get it going and show by modelling that it can and does work and is an effective additional tool in the teacher's tool bag.

But in terms of getting the approach to gain traction within your school, the identification of and support for those who will be advocates of independent learning is vital. As I said, there will always be those who are unsure or unwilling but there will also be those who are simply champing at the bit and ready to dive in. It is here that you will find your most willing supporters: teachers who are ready to experiment, spend the extra time that is needed to plan or re-plan their schemes of work, turn up to extra twilight sessions, volunteer to go on courses and generally speak out in favour of a new initiative. Carefully cultivated, these colleagues can become the first implementers, those who help to lead the way in the first phase of a new programme, and who can then in turn become supporters and trainers of others.

As I've been describing these change-leaders, you have probably already identified one or two colleagues who fit the description. Allocate time to work closely alongside them, meeting as regularly as possible, and trying to keep up conversations about how things are going, whether through formal meetings or through informal conversations over lunch or at break in the staffroom. If independent learning is going to become a central element in your school's approach to learning and teaching, you will need to establish a widening circle of teachers who understand, endorse and practise it in their classrooms.

Once you have identified enthusiastic advocates, think carefully about what you can do to support them. Can you allocate time to co-teach with them or observe them? Have you discussed plans for CPD with them? Can you share with them some of the responsibility of carrying out a pedagogical audit across the school?

Time spent with like-minded colleagues is time very well-spent, and it will provide you with the support you need as well, since implementing change across a school is always challenging and the encouragement that comes from ongoing conversations with others who share the vision is vital in maintaining the impetus for change.

Using your chief Socratic mentor: making use of experienced colleagues

I've suggested elsewhere (*Think Again: A Philosophical Approach to Teaching*) that every school has its own Socrates: a teacher who naturally teaches using the Socratic method of questioning and dialogue. This teacher will probably also be notable for their tendency to apply the same methodology to their interactions with colleagues and, taking a similar risk to Socrates himself, their superiors. In other words, they will often ask challenging, provocative questions, be insatiably curious about all sorts of topics and happiest when they are part of a group discussion rather than the sole voice of authority. They will tend to see connections between different topics and be interested in the bigger picture and the ethical questions raised by the things we teach children.

From the point of view of the development of independent learning within your school, teachers like this are a precious resource. I expect you identify with many of the character traits I've described and I imagine too that you can think of colleagues who also fit the bill. These are the people you should involve closely in the development of your programme for independent learning. They can be 'chief Socratic mentors' – teachers who take the lead in establishing a dialogue-led approach to teaching and learning and who are comfortable supervising students working on projects that range across different subject areas (something that often concerns teachers who are used to teaching only their own subject).

Work closely with your chief Socratic mentors, sharing with them the responsibility for training colleagues and overseeing the running of your independent learning initiatives. You may find, of course, that they will want to argue with you about the details of how these ventures are implemented, but that is no bad thing, and you will find that their philosophical approach makes them great role models for both students and other teachers.

Encouraging cautious adopters of change

When it comes to the development of independent learning, the majority of teachers fall into the 'willing but cautious' category. They will express support for the idea but also voice reservations, based on concerns about their own lack of experience or perception of the difficulty of finding space for independent learning in an already crowded curriculum.

The best way to address these concerns and to help them develop confidence is to listen carefully and then work out ways of involving them in the programme as supportively as possible. Their involvement can deepen as their knowledge and confidence grows, so to start with, you might want them simply to take on responsibility for supervising a few students, or co-facilitating discussion group activities. Some of the best outcomes occur when teachers who are initially sceptical get involved in a light-touch capacity, find out that it actually does work and then begin to imagine creative new ventures of their own.

If you are looking to spread a culture of independent learning throughout your school, you'll need to work with your senior leadership team to find a curriculum model that will allow most staff to get involved at some point and at some level. Don't make the mistake of confining the teaching to the 'dedicated few' who are the most eager adopters of independent learning; look at ways of bringing in the cautious-but-willing majority of your colleagues. This might be more of a medium-term planning goal, but it is important if you are going to diffuse the culture of independence across the whole curriculum.

Sharing best practice

As you work with colleagues, you will be providing guidance as well as observing examples of good practice. When it comes to dissemination, focus on how to get crucial messages shared with colleagues simply and swiftly. We are all busy and there are so many great ideas out there; what we need is access to direct, simple pointers about what will work. These can be provided in various ways:

- A quick conversation before a lesson.
- A brief chat to review a co-taught seminar.
- Recommendations of who to follow on Twitter.
- Emails with brief, bullet-pointed advice or links to great resources.
- A regular teaching-and-learning-focused item on the agenda for departmental meetings.
- Posters with suggestions on a teaching-and-learning noticeboard.

The emphasis when sharing best practice should be on providing ideas that are clear, simple and readily implementable.

Pause and think

What advice have you been given over the past term that you found really helpful?
What form did the advice come in?

Sharing plans and monitoring impact

Once you have a development plan in place, you will need to think about how to communicate it to colleagues and how to monitor impact. The main point I would urge is that we involve both teachers and students in the feedback process and that the focus for impact should be on attitudes towards learning.

A programme for developing independent learning will have succeeded if, and only if, students have developed greater confidence about managing their own learning. This can be assessed by looking at their performance, both in the context of project work and in other lessons, and also by looking for signs that their attitude towards learning has changed. We need independent learning because there is so much more to education that 'knowing the right answer'. We will know our approach is working when students begin to perceive this too and therefore take active responsibility for managing questions to which there is no obvious right answer.

Keeping it practical

One of the most important points of all about CPD is keeping it practical. I do a fair bit of CPD work myself, and I've sat through plenty of training sessions in my time. Looking back, the things that have worked best have been when the sessions are practically focused. It is when I'm trying to get something done and someone helps me to see how to do it better that I learn best.

When you've planned your CPD sessions, take a step back and look at the ratio of theoretical explanation to practical advice. I'm not saying we forget about theory entirely – but I do think we want to ensure we've stayed grounded in what we say. Aim for 80 to 90% practical advice.

Speaking from experience

The most useful advice I've received from colleagues has often been derived from their own experience. The great value of lessons learned from experience is that they are concrete and specific. No two students are the same, nor are two classes. Research evidence may provide us with a general framework to inform our approach but when it comes to knowing what will work well with a particular group of students, the experience of a colleague may be just the thing you need, especially if they have taught the very same group.

Whenever I'm running CPD sessions, I try to allow time for teachers to speak about what they have found has worked for them. I am not saying that we have to treat experience as the final word. We need to reflect on our experience in the light of theory and what research suggests. What is most effective is when experience and theory come together. So, for example, as we saw in chapter three, research indicates that project work has to be scaffolded. I often find that teachers' experience bears this out. When project work is begun without appropriate teaching beforehand, there are predictable difficulties. Conversely, talking about the importance of teaching prior to project work often leads to the sharing of good ideas about what works. Here, then, we have a happy marriage of experience and theory.

Effective examples: stories, illustrations and anecdotes

Bearing in mind the importance of backing up ideas with evidence drawn from experience, I would recommend building up a bank of stories and anecdotes to illustrate the points you make during professional development sessions. There is nothing so good as a story to help make a general point concrete and memorable.

Pause and think

Have a look at some TED talks given by teacher educators. How frequently do they draw heavily on anecdotes or stories? Of the talks you can remember, what makes them memorable?

As you develop your own programme for independent learning, you will have at your disposal a rich bank of stories on which to draw. It is worth getting feedback from both students and colleagues that you can weave into your CPD. Conducting an exit interview at the end of the course or even just inviting students to email you with their reflections on their experience can be helpful.

Make sure that you keep copies of all projects done by students. These are often very effective examples indeed, especially if the projects themselves include ongoing records of the process, which provide vivid examples of the power of independent learning to develop students' capacities for thinking for themselves.

Turning trainees into trainers

I am always delighted when teachers who have joined a programme of independent learning in order to find out how to do it move on to the stage where they are able to help train others.

I usually invite such teachers to participate in CPD sessions as co-trainers, perhaps asking them to speak about their own experience in a particular area. This is beneficial for them, helping to affirm their professional status as skilled practitioners, and of course, the preparation that goes into such training sessions is a valuable exercise in reflecting on practice. It can be fascinating to hear how ideas that you have taught colleagues, which they have taken up, used and adapted, are then explained by them to others. It reminds us that we should all continue learning from each other.

2 Training plans

Overview

What follows is a series of training plans for you to use when creating a training programme to help the teachers in your school develop their approach towards independent learning. They are organised as follows:

- Twilight session 1: Managing discussion in the classroom
- Twilight session 2: Socratic mentoring
- Twilight session 3: Teaching thinking skills
- Twilight session 4: Teaching research skills
- Twilight session 5: Developing project mentoring skills
- CPD INSET day: Pedagogical audit
- Mini twilight session series: Developing independent learning within subjects: (1) identifying obstacles, (2) identifying entry points, (3) managing progress, (4) assessment and evaluation.

A training plan is included here, and notes to accompany PowerPoint slides. The PowerPoints themselves can be downloaded from www.bloomsbury.com/CPD-library-independent-learning

Planning document

This table provides an overview of everything you need to know about the training sessions. One has been provided for each training session but there is also a template for the document online, which you can download and fill in, adapting to your own needs and context.

Below is an annotated example detailing what goes in each section.

Focus	Notes
Facilitators	*This section gets you thinking about whether there are any other members of staff who you might want to ask to help you with the training session.*
Topics covered	*The main topics covered in this training.*
Preparation tasks	*The main things you need to prepare for the training session.*
Resources required	*All the resources you need for the training session.*
Preparation time required	*A breakdown of the estimated amount of time you'll need to prepare for each session beforehand and on the day.*
Potential problems and solutions	*Problems to keep in mind that you might face with the training session and how you should deal with them.*
Possible follow-up tasks	*Activities, events or tasks that follow on nicely from the session that could be set up or completed.*
Pass it on	*Ideas for how to share the training with other teachers in the school, in other schools or across the country/world.*

Detailed presentation notes and PowerPoint slides

For each training session you are provided with detailed notes on each stage of the session, as well as a full set of PowerPoints for each session. These can be downloaded from www.bloomsbury.com/CPD-library-independent-learning and you can edit and adapt them to your context if required.

Before each session

For a session to run smoothly there needs to be some 'front-of-house' management. Depending on the numbers involved, you might want to ask a colleague to assist you with this. You'll need to ensure you are ready with your PowerPoint set up, the room laid out and handouts photocopied.

When thinking about the room layout, bear in mind that there are opportunities for discussion in all of the training sessions. Organising teachers into small groups around tables is a good idea, though if you do this, make sure they each have desk space for writing and can comfortably see the screen. A horseshoe arrangement is another possibility. If you are limited to working in a lecture format, with rows of chairs, check that teachers sit in a position where they can easily discuss with one or two others on either side of them.

Check that the screen is visible and run a check that the PowerPoint has loaded correctly.

For longer sessions, provide water at tables and schedule in breaks for refreshments and lunch.

It may be helpful to have name badges printed out.

It is worth trying to say hello to as many as possible of the delegates before the session formally begins. Often, they will have specific concerns or interests and you may find they are more willing to share these with you informally on a one-to-one basis.

I usually start a session with the formalities (a quick overview of the programme, when breaks will be, etc.) and then invite everyone present to briefly introduce themselves, and explain their interest and what they are hoping to get from the session. You might want to make brief notes as they speak, so you can ensure you've done your best to address their concerns. If you decide to start this way, make sure you introduce yourself as well, explaining how it is that you've become involved in work on independent learning.

Twilight session 1: Managing discussion in the classroom

Planning document

Focus	Notes
Facilitators	You may want to invite colleagues with whom you have worked closely and who will be able to share their own experience of independent learning.
Topics covered	• The role of discussion in forming independent learners. • What makes a good discussion starter. • Deep thinking questions. • Ground rules for classroom discussion.
Preparation tasks	• Organise the training room with an appropriate layout of chairs. • Check PowerPoint is running. • Print name badges if appropriate.
Resources required	• PowerPoint slides. • Data projector. • Flipchart/whiteboard and pens.
Preparation time required	• 30 minutes to check through PowerPoint. • 15 minutes to print out handouts. • 15 minutes to prepare room.
Potential problems and solutions	**Problem:** Some teachers may regard classroom discussion as having limited value for helping students learn. **Solution:** Think of examples from your own experience of classroom discussions that have worked well.
Possible follow-up tasks	Ask teachers to incorporate a discussion activity into a lesson in the coming week.
Pass it on	Ask teachers to share ideas for discussion topics with other members of their department.

Detailed session and preparation notes

PowerPoint required for this session: T1 Managing discussion in the classroom
www.bloomsbury.com/CPD-library-independent-learning

Aims and objectives *(Presentation and discussion)*

Spend a few minutes outlining the aims of the session. It is worth taking time here to ask people for their own initial reflections about independent learning and classroom discussion. This will give you a sense of what issues concern people most.

Slide 2: Aims and objectives

- Explore the role of classroom discussion in helping develop independent learning.
- Consider the type of question that starts a good discussion.
- Reflect on how to use discussion to facilitate deeper thinking.
- Discuss ground rules for classroom discussion.

The role of discussion in forming independent learners *(Presentation)*

Spend a few minutes explaining that independent learning is understood as a directed process, in which the teacher helps to create the conditions under which students can begin thinking for themselves. It may be helpful to explain that this conception of independent learning is one in which the teacher has a central role to play, as the catalyst for the process of thinking. Independent learning is not something that students will generally do naturally; they need to be prompted and guided. The thinking process begins when a question is asked that stimulates them to begin thinking and inquiring for themselves. We need therefore to consider the questions we ask, and assess their effectiveness as starting points for thinking. I suggest that the metaphor of 'flashpoint' questions can help here.

Slide 3: The role of discussion in forming independent learners

- Independent learning means teaching children to think for themselves.
- The key to getting children thinking is asking the right sort of question.
- The questions that spark discussion and debate – **flashpoint questions** – are the best starting points.

Trying out flashpoint questions *(Discussion and reflection)*

Ask teachers to break into groups (four to eight, ideally) and discuss one of the flashpoint questions (if they can think of an alternative question that would also work well, they are welcome to discuss that instead). After a few minutes of discussion, ask them to reflect on the conversation they have had, considering the nature of the thinking that took place, and reflecting on how successful the discussion was, and whether they can see this sort of conversation working in the classroom. If there is time, invite one person from each group to sum up their reflections on the discussion they have had.

Slide 4: Trying out flashpoint questions

Discuss: Choose one of the following questions for a five-minute group discussion:

- What is time?
- Can animals think?
- Is mathematics invented or discovered?
- Am I the same person as I was when I was born?

Reflect: After your discussion, reflect on how it went.

- What sort of thinking was going on?
- Did the questions work well as starting points for thinking?
- If so, what made them successful? If not, why not?

What makes a good discussion starter?
(Presentation and discussion)

Invite teachers to reflect on the features of questions that work well as starting points for discussion. Some questions we ask tend not to provoke much response; others seem to spark a reaction and lead to worthwhile discussion and debate. Worthwhile discussion starters usually have the features listed in the slide. The question links to the world of the students' own interests, knowledge and experience and usually it is open-ended, allowing for different possible answers.

Having explored these points, ask teachers to spend time in groups discussing what questions would work best for starting discussion in their subject area. This could be done as a think, pair, share exercise within the groups, with feedback to the whole group at the end.

Slide 5: What makes a good discussion starter?

Questions that work well for starting discussion have the following features:

Fertile   They stimulate thinking that leads to learning.
Accessible   They connect to the student's existing knowledge and experience.
Controversial There is more than one answer, interpretation or way of thinking about the question.
Engaging   The issue is interesting enough for students to want to discuss it.

Discuss: What questions would work well for starting discussion in your subject?

Deep thinking questions *(Presentation and discussion)*

We often ask questions where there is a right answer, and so there seems little point having further discussion. But beneath these closed questions lie a bunch of interesting, challenging, thought-provoking open questions about how we know what we know, and what it means. These are questions that call for deep thinking.

If our aim is to develop our students' capacity for independent thinking, we need to be prepared to press beyond the 'right answer' and challenge them to think about what knowledge is based on. This is a good technique for helping them develop as thinkers. It has also been shown to improve retention of knowledge. The evidence from educational psychology tells us that we remember what we have been made to think about. So, for example, following the question, 'How many degrees do the angles within a triangle add up to?', the next question might be: 'Why is that?' or 'How do you know?'

Ask teachers to get back into their groups and generate some deep thinking questions from their own subject area. Run the discussion using think, pair, share within small groups, then ask one or two from each group to provide one example each to the whole group.

Slide 6: Deep thinking questions

How do we keep students thinking even when they have found the right answer?

Good questions to ask include:

- How do you know?
- What is your argument for that?
- What is the evidence for that?
- Does anyone disagree? Why?
- What do you mean by... ?

Discuss: Take a topic from your subject and generate as many 'deep thinking' questions as you can about it.

Ground rules for classroom discussion *(Presentation)*

Up until now, the session has focused on what topics and questions work well. Many of the issues with running classroom discussion relate to problems of management; once the discussion has been started, what should we be doing to keep it on track? Spend a few minutes outlining the ground rules listed on slide 7. Teachers within the session may well have other pointers to share here.

Slide 7: Ground rules for classroom discussion

- Don't talk too much – be ready to listen.
- Give students time to think. Don't be afraid of silence.
- Use a carefully chosen stimulus.
- Invite students to respond to the comments of other students.
- Encourage students to back up their statements with arguments and evidence.
- Use different modes of discussion to boost participation and variety.
- As students become more confident, encourage them to take ownership of the discussion.

Classroom management *(Discussion)*

It is important that we remain realistic about the challenges of managing groups of students when they are engaged in discussion. The final slide invites teachers to reflect on the problems and challenges they face, and consider strategies for addressing them. You can run this discussion exercise by asking teachers to form small groups and then feed back.

Alternatively, depending on the size of your session, you may prefer to invite responses from teachers as part of a plenary discussion with the whole group.

It is worth emphasising the importance of careful preparation for classroom discussion, with points like the choice of stimulus, the layout of the room, the length of time you will allow for the discussion, and the format of the discussion needing consideration (some of these points were discussed in chapter five). There will be fewer problems if the topic chosen is one that the class finds interesting and accessible and if you arrange things so that everyone gets a chance to participate (using think, pair, share, for example).

Following this discussion, close the session by thanking teachers for their contributions and encouraging them to start trying out some of the ideas you have been discussing during the session. Remind them too that it is not 'all or nothing'; they can start small and grow from there. If they tend not to be confident about classroom discussion, a natural first step would be to plan one discussion activity to try out, as a starter or plenary, and go from there.

Slide 8: Classroom management

Discuss:

- What are the challenges with introducing classroom discussion?
- What classroom management challenges does it give rise to?
- How do you encourage quiet children to participate?
- How do you deal with children who go 'off-task'?

Twilight session 2: Socratic mentoring

Planning document

Focus	Notes
Facilitators	You may want to invite colleagues with whom you have worked closely and who will be able to share their own experience of Socratic mentoring.
Topics covered	• Being a Socratic mentor. • Exploring different types of discussion. • Forming a community of inquiry.
Preparation tasks	• Organise the training room with an appropriate layout of chairs. • Check PowerPoint is running. • Print name badges if appropriate.
Resources required	• PowerPoint slides. • Data projector. • Flipchart/whiteboard and pens.
Preparation time required	• 30 minutes to check through PowerPoint. • 15 minutes to print out handouts. • 15 minutes to prepare room.
Potential problems and solutions	**Problem:** Some teachers may not consider that their role is to provide mentoring to their students **Solution:** Explain the role of Socratic mentoring as a technique to be used alongside others.
Possible follow-up tasks	Ask teachers to incorporate a Socratic discussion into a lesson in the coming week.
Pass it on	Ask teachers to share their experience of Socratic mentoring with other members of their department.

Detailed session and preparation notes

PowerPoint required for this session: T2 Socratic mentoring www.bloomsbury.com/CPD-library-independent-learning

Aims and objectives *(Presentation and discussion)*

Spend a few minutes outlining the aims and objectives for the session. You might want to ask the teachers to give a brief summary of how they feel following the previous training session, where points about the management of classroom discussion were raised.

Slide 2: Aims and objectives

- Being a Socratic mentor.
- Exploring different types of discussion.
- Forming a community of inquiry.

Being a Socratic mentor *(Presentation and discussion)*

Socrates was famous for teaching by questioning, focusing particularly on the unexamined assumptions of his students, and on the significance of the topics they were discussing in relation to how life should be lived. He has become the role model for teachers who see their task as stimulating students to think for themselves, as opposed to 'telling them what they need to know'.

By no means do all teachers agree that they should be Socratic mentors. Even those who do see this as a role they should take on do not necessarily think it is their only role; students need to be instructed just as they need to be guided. The questions on this slide are designed to help teachers discuss the matter of how they see their role in an open fashion.

Slide 3: Being a Socratic mentor

- Teaching by asking questions.
- Challenging assumptions.
- Exploring the uncertain and paradoxical elements of learning.
- Linking learning to life.

Exploring different types of discussion
(Presentation and discussion)

Classroom discussion can serve different purposes. The three listed on this slide vary in the extent to which they are teacher-directed. Socratic questioning often involves the teacher posing the questions, with the student being led towards a final answer that the teacher has in mind. The second discussion type involves setting up the class as a 'community of inquiry', the aim of which is for students to participate in a shared investigation of a topic, with some guidance and facilitation from the teacher. A third stage is for a conversation to be fully democratic, with the teacher participating on an equal footing with the students. This might be achieved by one of the students being asked to initiate and chair the discussion, for example, with the teacher observing (and only interjecting if necessary, to steer the discussion back on course, or if classroom management issues arise).

There is no right answer to the question of which of these types of discussion is 'best'. They serve different purposes. The point could be made, though, in discussing the question on this slide, that there are times when the teacher clearly is an expert, and other times, as when controversial ethical or philosophical questions arise, when the teacher cannot legitimately claim expertise.

Slide 4: Exploring different types of discussion

- **Socratic questioning:** Using questions as a path to a conclusion.
- **Community of inquiry:** A group investigation of a topic with the teacher as facilitator.
- **Democratic discussion:** An open exchange of ideas with the teacher as an equal participant.

Discuss:

o   What are the challenges posed by each of these?
o   How comfortable are you using these in the classroom?
o   'If the teacher is the expert, democratic discussion is not really possible.' Do you agree?

Forming a community of inquiry *(Group discussion)*

The training session ends with group discussion, the purpose of which is to learn about what it feels like to participate in a community of inquiry and for the teachers concerned to reflect on how such discussions could be held in the classroom. It may be instructive to ask the facilitator to comment on how they found the discussion.

Slide 5: Forming a community of inquiry

Group discussion:

- Generate a series of questions on the topic of 'childhood'.
- Choose one question.
- With one member of the group acting as a facilitator, hold a community of inquiry discussion of the question.
- Finally, reflect on the challenges of running a discussion of this type in the classroom.

Twilight session 3: Teaching thinking skills

Planning document

Focus	Notes
Facilitators	You may want to invite colleagues with whom you have worked closely and who will be able to share their own experience of independent learning.
Topics covered	• Creating time to think. • Using logic as a thinking tool. • Effective pre-study. • Obstacles to thinking and how to deal with them.
Preparation tasks	• Organise the training room with an appropriate layout of chairs. • Check PowerPoint is running. • Print name badges if appropriate.
Resources required	• PowerPoint slides. • Data projector. • Flipchart/whiteboard and pens.
Preparation time required	• 30 minutes to check through PowerPoint. • 15 minutes to print out handouts. • 15 minutes to prepare room.
Potential problems and solutions	**Problem:** Some teachers may not appreciate the value of teaching students to think for themselves. **Solution:** Explain the role of thinking in helping students retain knowledge, learn more deeply and cope with complexity.
Possible follow-up tasks	Ask teachers to incorporate a thinking catalyst activity into a lesson in the coming week.
Pass it on	Ask teachers to share ideas for getting students thinking with other members of their department.

Detailed session and preparation notes

PowerPoint required for this session: T3 Teaching thinking skills www.bloomsbury.com/CPD-library-independent-learning

Aims and objectives *(Presentation and discussion)*

Spend a few minutes outlining the aims and objectives for the session. You might want to ask the teachers to give a brief explanation of the way they teach thinking skills and what they are hoping to gain from the session.

Slide 2: Aims and objectives

- Creating time to think.
- Using logic as a thinking tool.
- Effective pre-study.
- Obstacles to thinking and how to deal with them.

Can students be taught to think? *(Presentation and discussion)*

The teaching of thinking skills is the subject of ongoing discussion and debate, and it is worth beginning the session by asking teachers to discuss the question of whether students can in fact be taught to think, whether it is a natural aptitude, or whether learning to think happens as a by-product of teaching a subject. Having had some initial discussion of this, it is worth noting that there are particular techniques that can be helpful in facilitating the process of thinking, and these will form the focus of the training session.

Slide 3: Can students be taught to think?

Discuss:

- o Can you teach a student to think?
- o Is the ability to think a natural aptitude?
- o Is learning to think better a by-product of learning a subject?

Learning by thinking *(Presentation and discussion)*

Spend a few minutes outlining some of the findings of educational researchers about the close link between learning and thinking (see chapter three for more details). The discussion questions are designed to provide an opportunity for teachers to think about thinking. Sometimes, it can be quite simple points that need to be addressed, such as the importance of allowing time for students to think before answering, the need to encourage students to try ideas out without fear of being wrong, or the basic point of why we want them to think things through, rather than simply wait for the teacher to tell them the answers.

Slide 4: Learning by thinking

- One of the clearest findings of educational research is that there is a close relationship between thinking and learning.
- 'Learning happens when people have to think hard.' (Professor Robert Coe)
- 'Memory is the residue of thought.' (Professor Daniel Willingham)

Discuss:

- o How important is thinking as part of the learning process?
- o Do our students have time to think?
- o What do we need to change if we are to encourage more thinking within our classrooms?

Using logic as a thinking tool *(Presentation and discussion)*

One thing that we can do to help students think better is to assist them in the organisation of their thoughts. A framework for organising their thoughts is provided in this slide. It can be used to help give structure to a class discussion, or as a framework for essay writing or project work. Spend time discussing the value of having a logical structure, and ask teachers to consider activities that can help students develop their ability to reason logically. Often, the first step is simply identifying whether a statement is expressing a point of view or providing evidence in support of a conclusion. The sort of exercise students can work on includes taking a newspaper article and identifying the main point of view, the arguments and the counter-arguments. If there is time, you could choose a suitable article and run this activity as an exercise for the teachers in the session.

Slide 5: Using logic as a thinking tool

- Logic is the study of the structure of arguments.
- A simple logical model of the argument process goes like this:
  - o point of view
  - o argument
  - o counter-argument
  - o response.

Discuss:

> o How can logic be used as a tool for facilitating classroom discussions?
> o How can logic be used to provide a framework to assist students with their essay writing?
> o What exercises could you use in the classroom to help students develop their logical reasoning skills?

Effective pre-study *(Presentation and discussion)*

Students need help with the organisation of their thinking; but they also need to have something to think about. Pre-study is a technique that can help to lead to more thoughtful, informed classroom discussions. Have a look at the details provided in chapter five about the different forms of pre-study. The technique tends to work best if there is an accessible stimulus article, or if the basis for the discussion is material that the student has worked on and with which they are familiar. Spend some time discussing how this approach could be used, and how an existing unit of study could be adapted to include it.

Slide 6: Effective pre-study

- Study prior to classroom discussion has a valuable role to play in helping students learn to think better.
- Contexts for pre-study include:
  - o student-led seminars
  - o work-in-progress seminars
  - o student presentation.

Discuss:

> o Choose a unit of study and discuss how you could incorporate pre-study as a technique for enriching students' thinking. What types of subject matter lend themselves to this approach?

Obstacles to thinking and how to deal with them
(Presentation and discussion)

The final few minutes of the training session should be spent inviting teachers to reflect on the challenge of getting students to think. It will not be difficult to identify a series of obstacles. If teachers are struggling to identify steps that could be taken to address these, try reversing the question, and ask them to think back to lessons that they have taught during which they would say that students were thinking well. What made those lessons work? It is often quite simple things that make the difference. If the question that is chosen as the stimulus is challenging yet accessible, if there are obvious alternative possible answers and if it is sufficiently interesting for students to want to make the effort to work out an answer, then it is more likely that it will result in thinking.

Slide 7: Obstacles to thinking and how to deal with them

Discuss:

- Make a list of the things that impede thinking in the classroom (e.g. time pressure, lack of confidence, complexity of the material...).
- Organise the list into order, with the most pressing difficulties at the top.
- Discuss each in turn. Have you had any experience of dealing with the difficulties? What strategies would be worth trying?

Twilight session 4: Teaching research skills

Planning document

Focus	Notes
Facilitators	You may want to invite colleagues with whom you have worked closely and who will be able to share their own experience of teaching research skills.
Topics covered	• Getting started with research. • Moving beyond searching. • Creating a plan of research. • Teaching research by research.
Preparation tasks	• Organise the training room with an appropriate layout of chairs. • Check PowerPoint is running. • Print name badges if appropriate.
Resources required	• Access to enough computers for teachers to work in pairs on a project. • PowerPoint slides. • Data projector. • Flipchart/whiteboard and pens.
Preparation time required	• 30 minutes to check through PowerPoint. • 15 minutes to print out handouts. • 15 minutes to prepare room.
Potential problems and solutions	**Problem:** Some teachers may not feel that there is much point trying to get students to research. **Solution:** Explain the value of teaching students to learn by making their own inquiries.
Possible follow-up tasks	Ask teachers to incorporate a research activity into a lesson in the coming week.
Pass it on	Ask teachers to share ideas for getting students researching with other members of their department.

Detailed session and preparation notes

PowerPoint required for this session: T4 Teaching Research Skills www.bloomsbury.com/CPD-library-independent-learning

Aims and objectives *(Presentation and discussion)*

Spend a few minutes outlining the aims and objectives for the session. You might want to ask the teachers to give a brief explanation of the way they teach research skills and what they are hoping to gain from the session. This session involves a practical exercise in which teachers are asked to begin a small research project then share with the rest of the group some of the lessons learned.

Slide 2: Aims and objectives

- Getting started with research.
- Moving beyond searching.
- Creating a plan of research.
- Teaching research by research.

Getting started with research *(Discussion)*

Allow a few minutes for group discussion with feedback. The object of the discussion is to explore ideas about classroom research exercises in a preliminary fashion. The third question alludes to the problem that students tend to think that research means little more than finding information using an online search, a point explored in the next slide.

Slide 3: Getting started with research

Discuss:

- What opportunities are there for research in your subject?
- What difficulties do students face when they are asked to research?
- What can you do to stop research exercises turning into 'cut and paste'?

Moving beyond searching *(Presentation)*

Research may begin with the search for information but it does not end there. The challenge is to take the information, explore its meaning (analysis), make connections between points (synthesis) and form an opinion about its quality (evaluation). One way of getting students to engage with these aspects of the research process is to ask them to write up their research as a story, with a coherent progression of ideas linking the different elements (an idea explored in chapter five).

Slide 4: Moving beyond searching

- There is more to researching than just searching.
- Collection of information needs to be followed by analysis, synthesis and evaluation.
- Writing up research as a story is better than simply assembling information.

Good research questions *(Discussion)*

As with classroom discussion, so with research: the inquiry will work best if it begins with a suitable question. What makes a good research question? Ask teachers to discuss in groups, then feed back. The features of good research questions are more or less the same as those of good discussion starters (you may remember the FACE acronym from the training session on managing classroom discussion: Fertile, Accessible, Controversial, Engaging). Rather than simply stating these points, allow ideas to emerge from the group; it is likely that these features will be mentioned.

Slide 5: Good research questions

- Effective research begins with a good question.

Discuss:

    o What are the features of good research questions?

Creating a plan of research *(Presentation and discussion)*

Discuss the value of a plan of research. Students can very quickly get lost when they are engaging in research. It helps enormously to have a plan in place, so that as new material is explored, the findings can be slotted into an already-existent structure (which can, of course, be modified as they learn more). Thinking about the sub-headings that they would use to structure a research report is a good way of creating a plan. Allow teachers time to invent a question, write a research plan, then reflect on how they would do this with one of their classes.

Slide 6: Creating a plan of research

- A plan of research helps students to keep control of the research process and produce a well-organised research review.
- Initial research is needed to establish a series of headings (which can be in the form of sub-questions) for the research review.

Discuss:

- o Pick a topic that you teach, choose a research question, then make a plan of research.
- o Reflect on how you would teach students to do this.

Teaching research by research *(Group research exercise)*

Teaching research skills to students whilst they are actually researching makes far more sense than making them sit through a research methods course before letting them get started. A small 'pilot' project provides a good context for teaching students how to find, analyse and write up information from sources. One of the most useful things to learn is just how helpful computers can be: tasks like creating citations, bibliographies, tables of contents and headings are easier than ever, thanks to technology. Some teachers will be familiar with these tools; for those who aren't, even just a few minutes experimentation (with the aid of the 'help' function if necessary) will show them how to use them. I suggest that around half the session is given over to letting teachers practise creating a small project of their own, exploring the research tools on the computer as they do and looking as well for good quality sources. Time spent here is time well-spent, as it doesn't take long to discover some really useful tools. Finally, bring them back together to for a 'show and tell' session.

Slide 7: Teaching research by research

- The best context for teaching research skills is a small-scale pilot project (around 1,000 words).

Group exercise: create a pilot project

- o Spend the remainder of the session working with a partner to plan and begin a small-scale pilot project on a question of your choosing.
- o As part of your project, experiment with the tools provided on your computer for creating headings, citations, bibliographies and tables of contents.
- o Look for easy-to-access, high-quality research sources.
- o In the final few minutes of the session, share what you have learned with the rest of the group.

Twilight session 5: Developing project mentoring skills

Planning document

Focus	Notes
Facilitators	You may want to invite colleagues with whom you have worked closely and who will be able to share their own experience as project mentors.
Topics covered	• What is a project? • Teaching for project work. • Choosing good titles. • Developing project ideas. • Pilot projects. • Steps to success. • Challenges.
Preparation tasks	• Organise the training room with an appropriate layout of chairs. • Check PowerPoint is running. • Print name badges if appropriate.
Resources required	• PowerPoint slides. • Data projector. • Flipchart/whiteboard and pens.
Preparation time required	• 30 minutes to check through PowerPoint. • 15 minutes to print out handouts. • 15 minutes to prepare room.
Potential problems and solutions	**Problem:** Some teachers may feel that project work doesn't fit into their subject area. **Solution:** Emphasise the variety of forms that project work can take and that it can run on different time scales, ranging from one or two weeks through to a whole year.
Possible follow-up tasks	Ask teachers to plan to incorporate project work into a forthcoming unit.
Pass it on	Ask teachers to share ideas for project topics with other members of their department.

Detailed session and preparation notes

PowerPoint required for this session: T5 Developing project mentoring skills
www.bloomsbury.com/CPD-library-independent-learning

Aims and objectives *(Presentation and discussion)*
Spend a few minutes outlining the aims and objectives for the session. You might want to ask the teachers to give a brief explanation of their own use of project work, and what they are hoping to gain from the session.

Slide 2: Aims and objectives

- Considering the nature of projects.
- Reflecting on the teaching that is needed as a foundation for project work.
- Reflecting on what makes a good project title.
- Making use of pilot projects.
- Exploring what makes the project process work successfully.
- Considering challenges.

What is a project? *(Presentation)*

The term 'project' is used in different ways. For the purposes of this session, we are defining it as a process of creation, or inquiry, driven by a personally chosen goal (a question to be investigated, or a practical aim to be achieved). It is worth emphasising that it is more than just a simple task: carrying out a project is a process that has recognisable phases, including planning, researching, developing and reviewing.

This is also a good time to explore the value of project work. As a vehicle for allowing students to explore more deeply, and learn more independently, project work is hard to beat. But it needs proper stage-setting; hence the place to begin is with a discussion of what we need to teach students in order to equip them for project work.

Slide 3: What is a project?

- A project is a personally chosen process of inquiry or creation.
- It is not just a task.
- Projects involve the phases of planning, researching, developing and reviewing.
- Projects enable deeper learning because they allow students to exercise freedom of choice and provide time for them to develop their ideas.
- Successful projects depend on a basis of ideas and skills provided through teaching.

Teaching for project work *(Presentation and discussion)*

Introduce the point about teaching by referring to two elements that students need before they begin project work: skills and ideas. They need to have some idea of what sort of question is worth asking, and what sort of practical challenge they can realistically undertake, and they need to have skills in areas such as researching, developing their own ideas and presenting their work.

Ask teachers to discuss the way they would go about preparing students for project work. The discussion can happen in small groups, with feedback to the large group.

In summing up this section of the session, you might want to refer to some of the research summarised in chapter three that highlights the difference between 'unguided discovery' and 'scaffolded' project work, with the evidence favouring the latter approach.

Slide 4: Teaching for project work

- Project skills need to be taught.
- Students need to explore ideas so that they can make meaningful choices when it comes to selecting their project title.

Discussion:

- If you are going to run a project as part of a unit of study, what skills and ideas do you need to teach beforehand as a foundation?

Choosing good titles *(Discussion and reflection)*

The choice of title is clearly a vital part of the project process. Allow time for teachers to generate project ideas then reflect on these, thinking about what makes the difference between good and bad titles. Depending on numbers, this is likely to work best with small discussion groups, with feedback from one or two in the group at the end of the discussion.

Following discussion, highlight the points made on slide 6 about the features of good titles. It is worth emphasising the value of open-ended questions or practical challenges; it is when there is more than one alternative answer or design that the student needs to begin thinking about which of the options is best, and this means that they will be thinking more deeply about their work than if they were simply summarising ideas based on research.

Slide 5: Choosing good titles

Discussion:

- Generate a list of ideas for projects linked to your subject.

Reflect:

- Discuss what makes the difference between a good and bad title.

Slide 6: Good titles

- The choice of project title is important and should not be rushed.
- Titles should be negotiated with the mentor.

The best titles have the following features:

- personally interesting
- researchable
- specific
- open-ended
- suitably pitched.

Developing project ideas *(Discussion)*

This discussion exercise is designed to bring together some of the points that will have been explored about good titles. The ideas on the slide are promising, but also quite broad in scope. The general direction that students need to take will be towards more specifically defined objectives. Questions such as who they are producing their work for, what effect they want to achieve and how they will measure success can help to provide this focus.

Allow time for teachers to discuss then share their thoughts with others in the session.

Slide 7: Developing project ideas

Discussion:

- How would you advise a student who wants to do a community project?
- What would you say to a student who wanted to do a music project?
- How would you advise a student who wants to develop a project based on their sports training programme?

A template for a project report *(Presentation)*

Getting a good structure in place is very helpful as a way of helping students proceed through the project process. The template presented here can be used to help students organise their final report. It contains sections corresponding to the different phases of the project process: first, students write a plan, then begin a journal (a record of the project process, where they can provide background information about their activities, thoughts and decisions). When it comes to the report itself, the natural place to begin is with the research, then the development section, followed by the introduction (which is best written after they have produced most of the report, and have a clearer idea of what it is all about). A review of the project process and a bibliography round things out.

Slide 8: A template for a project report

- Plan
- Project journal
- Introduction
- Research
- Development
- Review
- Bibliography

Getting going *(Discussion)*

This discussion activity is designed to provide teachers with an opportunity to think through the transition from an initial idea to a clearly defined project title and from there into the project itself. The key point to discuss is how to help the student take these initial steps. Clearly the student will need to do some initial research, then come up with a proper plan for the project. It is worth discussing what areas of research should be included in the plan and what sort of question or practical goal might emerge.

This exercise will work as a small group discussion, with one person per group providing brief feedback.

Slide 9: Getting going

Discussion:

- You have a student who has decided they would like to do a project on video games. How would you advise them to get started?

Pilot projects *(Presentation)*

A pilot project is a valuable training exercise that can be used prior to commencing work on a longer project. For example, if a class is going to be assigned a five-week project, the first week can be set aside for a pilot. Talk through the points on slide 10, and explain that a pilot project can be helpful as a way of allowing students to move into project work in a supported environment, and to try out ideas that they may or may not want to take forward into the full project.

Slide 10: Pilot projects

- A short warm-up exercise before the real thing.
- Student chooses question, finds sources and reviews them.
- A chance to teach research techniques (e.g. using citations, constructing bibliographies, evaluating sources).
- Short summative oral presentation and report.

Steps to success with projects *(Presentation)*

Talk through these points fairly briskly, but allow time for questions or comments from teachers in the session. If you can think of examples from your own experience, so much the better (or have a look back at chapter four for further discussion of the mentoring process).

The crucial point about project work is the need to find and keep momentum. So long as students do a little more work on their project each lesson, things will keep moving forward. The main role of the project mentor is to make it easy to take the next step, and to be ready to intervene if it looks as though the project has stalled.

Slide 11: Steps to success with projects

- The best way to write the project is to write the project!
- Create a plan of research.
- Check title (focus, research base, open-ended).
- Agree deadlines.
- Fine-tune the title following research.
- Keep process records.
- Write a research review (analysis of sources).
- Develop arguments using source material.
- Consider counter-arguments/alternative views.
- Hold regular supervised sessions.
- Review drafts and allow time for re-drafting.
- Maintain a supervisor's log.
- End process with an oral presentation/Q and A.

Challenges *(Discussion)*

The plenary discussion exercise provides an opportunity for teachers to air their concerns and share ideas about how to carry out the exciting but challenging work of being a project mentor. In my experience, the challenges of project work are largely the same, regardless of the type of project, and so you can expect teachers to want to discuss issues such as how to find time for project work alongside everything else that has to be taught, what to do with students who lose motivation, how to help when a student picks a topic that is outside the teacher's own area of subject expertise, how much assistance to offer and what to do if a student wants to change their title.

It is worth emphasising that project work happens best with regular guidance from the project mentor; just as students need to be taught to think independently, they need to be taught how to go through the different phases of the project process, and supervised as they do. Many of the challenges can be met, or at least minimised, by ensuring that there is regular communication between student and project mentor.

Slide 12: Challenges

Discussion:

- What would you identify as the main challenges when it comes to implementing project work and how can you address them?

CPD INSET day: Pedagogical audit

Planning document

Focus	Notes
Facilitators	You may want to co-lead the session with a colleague who has also been exploring how to embed independent learning in their day-to-day teaching.
Topics covered	• What is pedagogical audit? • Different discussion formats. • Using discussion groups to stimulate thinking. • Techniques for developing independence in the classroom. • Planning for independence.
Preparation tasks	• Organise the training room with an appropriate layout of chairs. • Check PowerPoint is running. • Print name badges if appropriate.
Resources required	• PowerPoint slides. • Data projector • Flipchart/whiteboard and pens. • You may want to select a stimulus article for use in one of the discussion activities. Teachers will be asked to revise a lesson plan/scheme of work – it may be helpful if they have selected these in advance of the session.
Preparation time required	• 30 minutes to check through PowerPoint. • 15 minutes to print out handouts. • 15 minutes to prepare room.
Potential problems and solutions	**Problem:** Some teachers may see little point in trying to develop independent learning. **Solution:** Think of examples from your own experience of how independent learning can be embedded within day-to-day teaching, and the benefits that ensue.
Possible follow-up tasks	Ask teachers to plan further lessons that feature independent learning for use in the coming week.
Pass it on	Ask teachers to share their experience of independent learning with other members of their department.

Detailed session and presentation notes

PowerPoint required for this session: INSET Day: Pedagogical audit www.bloomsbury.com/CPD-library-independent-learning

Aims and objectives *(Presentation and discussion)*

This session is designed for a whole-staff INSET day, or part of such a day. The main aim is to help all teachers to appreciate that they can weave independent learning into their day-to-day teaching, alongside the other teaching approaches they use. The tool for doing this is 'pedagogical audit', which involves taking a look at a lesson plan or a scheme of work, spotting openings where independent learning can be incorporated, and planning the activities that will enable this to happen.

Depending on how much time is available, you might like to work through the training material on pedagogical audit, discussion and techniques for developing independence during morning sessions, leaving the afternoon free for teachers to work on planning lessons and schemes of work, with a plenary session when everyone reconvenes to review what they have come up with.

If time is tight, you could leave the planning to be done following the CPD day. If so, it would be worth arranging an alternative forum for ideas to be reflected on, perhaps through short contributions to departmental meetings.

Assuming you are going to run the whole session, begin by asking teachers to talk to a partner for a minute or two about the points, if any, in their current teaching when they feel they do make use of independent learning. You might ask for a few of the teachers attending the session to share their answers with the whole group, then go on to explain the aims of the session, which centre on finding points within our day-to-day teaching where we can create space for students to develop as independent learners. The emphasis is on independent learning as a natural part of the learning of any subject, not as some isolated 'bolt-on' subject that happens only through special project assignments, for example.

Slide 2: Aims and objectives

- Explore pedagogical audit and its role in helping move towards independent learning on a whole-school basis.
- Explore the use of different formats for discussion in order to stimulate thinking.
- Discuss techniques for developing independence in the classroom.
- Lesson planning and reviewing schemes of work to promote independent learning.

What is pedagogical audit? *(Presentation)*

Spend a few minutes introducing the idea of pedagogical audit. Emphasise that this is a tool for enabling the incorporation of independent learning within each subject. Most teachers already incorporate some discussion activities and some project assignments, and expect some independent reading and research to be done. The question is: can we find space for more of this sort of thing?

Slide 3: What is pedagogical audit?

- **Pedagogical audit** is a process of reviewing a scheme of work or series of lesson plans with the aim of including more activities that promote independent learning.
- Specifically, this includes using *discussions, project work* and *techniques for creating thinking time in lessons.*

Different discussion formats *(Presentation)*

Discussion in the classroom has a vital role to play in developing independent learning. Take some time to explore some of the different formats that can be used. Take a look back at part 1 for more background information on these formats. It is worth emphasising the value of using different types of discussion; this will add variety to lessons (always a good thing) and help to ensure that more students are drawn into discussions.

The formats listed on this slide can function in different ways to help meet specific challenges that arise when we seek to engage our classes in discussion. For example, think, pair, share works very well indeed when a question is first introduced because it provides all students with an opportunity to get involved in the discussion by speaking to their partner, even if they are reluctant to then share with the whole class. The technique also involves a deliberate focus on pausing to get time for students to think before they speak; something we all too easily omit when we question classes as a whole.

Slide 4: Different discussion formats

- class debate
- think, pair, share
- question-bouncing
- fish bowl
- work-in-progress seminar
- student presentation.

Using discussion groups to stimulate thinking
(Discussion and reflection)

It is worth taking time to try out some of the discussions, in groups of six to eight teachers in each. On slide 5, I've suggested two topics for discussion; you can use these or another of your own choosing if you prefer. You could also find a stimulus article that the group could read before the discussion activity. I'd suggest as well that you ask one of the group to facilitate the discussion, perhaps beginning by giving a brief overview of the stimulus article.

It is important to allow time to reflect on how the discussions went: what sort of thinking was going on? Did the teachers in the group find that they were helped or hindered in developing their own ideas by the presence of others? What challenges did the facilitator encounter? Could they see activities like this happening in their lessons and if so, what issues would be likely to arise?

I would suggest you allow a good ten minutes for each discussion, a further five for reflection and some time for one of the group members to feed back to everyone else. It is probably best to take the discussion activities one at a time, with reflection and feedback in between.

Slide 5: Using discussion groups to stimulate thinking

Discussions:

- In groups, run the following discussion activities:
  - A seminar discussion on the statement 'Imagination is more important than knowledge'.
  - A 'think, pair, share' discussion on the question 'Can bad people create good art?'

Reflection:

- Discuss how these activities would work in the classroom. What challenges would you face and how would you address them?

Techniques for developing independence in the classroom
(Presentation and discussion)

One of the biggest challenges we face in trying to develop independent learning is that there is so much to get through. How do we find time for it? The techniques listed on slide 6 are designed to provide routes for weaving independent learning in alongside our existing teaching, or making some changes to what we do so that there is more scope for students to take the lead. Take time to explain how these different techniques work (for more detail, see part 1 of the book). If you can, provide examples from your own experience.

Allow time for teachers to discuss how these techniques can be woven into their teaching. It is worth reminding them that these changes can be quite small: interspersing some peer instruction during a lesson, for example, or asking students to take the lead in teaching a revision class. Projects too need not last for weeks and weeks; they could be factored in alongside a taught unit, using some lessons for project work and some homework time.

Slide 6: Techniques for developing independence in the classroom

- learning-based projects
- collaborative research

- deeper-thinking review lessons
- big problem lessons
- peer instruction
- student teaching
- flipped schemes of work
- student-led seminars.

Discussion:

- What project ideas could you weave into your teaching?
- Where are there opportunities for you to get students researching more?

Planning for independence
(Presentation, planning, discussion and review)

This slide introduces some activities that could occupy a substantial portion of the CPD day: a full afternoon, for example. The aim is to encourage colleagues to take a lesson or a scheme of work that they are about to teach and carry out a pedagogical audit on it, looking at how some of the techniques for developing independence can be incorporated.

The activities will probably work best if teachers pair up with a colleague from their department. Allow plenty of time for them to select, discuss and revise their plans and schemes of work. Allow time as well for them to reconvene as a group (again, six to eight is about the right group size) and share the work they've done. This will provide a good opportunity for the sharing of ideas and for peer review. It is also always of interest to teachers to find out what their colleagues in other departments are getting up to!

Slide 7: Planning for independence

- Write a plan for a lesson using some of the techniques for developing independence.
- Share with colleagues and discuss the challenges of teaching in this way.
- Review a scheme of work for a unit you will soon be teaching. What elements can you include that will help develop independence (class discussion, projects, flipped learning, etc.)?
- Present your ideas to colleagues and discuss your revised scheme.

Mini-session series: Embedding independent learning within subjects

Planning document

Focus	Notes
Facilitators	These mini-sessions could be run by heads of subject areas with their own departments.
Topics covered	• Identifying obstacles. • Identifying entry points. • Managing progress. • Assessment and evaluation.
Preparation tasks	• Organise the training room with an appropriate layout of chairs. • Check PowerPoint is running.
Resources required	• PowerPoint slides. • Data projector. • Flipchart/whiteboard and pens.
Preparation time required	• 15 minutes to check through PowerPoint and background to the session. • Five minutes to prepare room.
Potential problems and solutions	**Problem:** Some teachers may regard independent learning as irrelevant to their day-to-day teaching. **Solution:** Show how the starting points for developing independent learning already exist within regular classroom activities.
Possible follow-up tasks	Ask teachers to report back on how things are going with their own exploration of independent learning.
Pass it on	Ask teachers to lead a 'teaching and learning' slot in a future meeting with other members of their department.

Detailed session and presentation notes

PowerPoint required for this session: Mini sessions: Embedding independent learning within subjects www.bloomsbury.com/ CPD-library-independent-learning

This series is designed to explore teachers as they work within their departments to embed independent learning within their subject area. It comprises a series of short, 15-minute CPD sessions, which could be run as stand-alone sessions, during weekly departmental meetings, or a mini-twilight session. There is material for four mini-sessions, though these could easily be combined into two longer sessions, or even a single session.

It is not necessary for you to run these yourself; they are designed to enable a head of a department to lead a session with their team. The focus of the sessions is on professional reflection; there is not a great deal of information to be presented. They will function best as focal points for discussion and thinking about implementation once the other training sessions have run, and teachers have some familiarity with independent learning as we have been defining it and the kind of activities that help to make it happen within the classroom. Suppose, for example, that you have run the training sessions on discussion, project work and pedagogical audit within the first two terms of an academic year. These mini-sessions could be used for consolidation during the third term, a time in the year when teachers will often be turning their thoughts to their plans for the subsequent academic year, and therefore ready to explore making adjustments to their approach.

Remember that the focus throughout all the training you provide is on helping teachers to see independent learning not as something completely new and alien but as an extension of and development from their day-to-day teaching. We all give students some degree of independence, some space to think, decide and experiment for themselves. These mini-sessions are designed to help teachers think, in practical terms, about how they can give students more freedom to think for themselves.

Aims and objectives *(Presentation)*

This slide introduces the series of mini-sessions. Use it to introduce each session, then jump to the appropriate slide on the PowerPoint. It is worth explaining how these mini-sessions relate to the other training sessions, the idea being that having learned about techniques for developing independent learning, teachers can think in more detail about how they apply this within their own subject. This sort of thinking will have begun if they have followed the training session on the pedagogical audit process but they will probably not have had much opportunity to explore the challenges and opportunities as a subject team. This is the purpose of these mini-sessions.

Slide 2: Aims and objectives for mini-sessions

- Identifying obstacles.
- Identifying entry points.
- Managing progress.
- Assessment and evaluation.

Identifying obstacles *(Discussion)*

Slide 3 of the presentation can be used to start a discussion about the obstacles to developing independent learning and the ways that these can be addressed. In preparing to lead the discussion, it might be helpful to revisit the start of part 2 of this book ('Challenges for trainers'), where some of the most commonly encountered obstacles to independent learning are described, with some brief suggestions about possible responses.

It is worth keeping in mind that, as with any proposed development, there will be some teachers who are eager to embrace change, others who are cautious and a number who may simply be implacably opposed. The key to helping move things forward is to keep explaining the reasons why it matters that students learn independently, and to show how readily and easily it is possible to begin to move in the direction of increasing their independence, never forgetting that some will go further along this path than others.

Depending on the size of the group of teachers in this session, it may be best to run the discussion as a whole group, or as a think, pair, share exercise.

Slide 3: Identifying obstacles

Discussion:

- What are the obstacles to developing more independent learning in your subject area?
- What options do you have for addressing these?

Identifying entry points *(Discussion)*

This mini-session is designed to help a department reflect on its approach to teaching, perhaps during a phase of curriculum review. If teachers look blank when the discussion questions are posed, remind them of some of the ideas highlighted in the CPD session on managing classroom discussion, about the type of question that functions well as a starting point for discussion, and the suggestions made in the session on pedagogical audit about techniques that can be used to develop independence.

The mini-session should not require a long presentation; ideally, teachers will discuss amongst themselves and begin to spot opportunities. In keeping with the theme of this book (that we teach students to become independent), it is natural to look, initially at least, at gaps towards the end of units of study. Could independent research be included as a synoptic activity at the end of a unit, for example? Is there a gap following exams that could be filled by a project?

Slide 4: Identifying entry points

Discussion:

- Where, within your subject, is there scope for you to introduce more independent learning?
- What steps should you take to make this happen?

Managing progress *(Discussion)*

This mini-session is intended to help teachers think through some of the practical challenges of acting as a 'Socratic mentor'. What does it mean, in practical terms, to take on the role of a facilitator of independent learning? Some of the key points that are likely to come up in the discussion were explored in the CPD session on project mentoring, and discussed in chapter four. If you are leading this session, you might like to review these beforehand.

The point of the second question is to direct attention to the preparations that need to go on before independent learning activities are assigned to students. 'Resources' here include materials that they might need for practical tasks, IT resources, research sources that they may need access to and the all-important resource of teacher time; given that they will need to be supervised on a regular basis for progress to be maintained, how will you find time? The idea of micro-tutorials, discussed in chapter four, may be helpful here.

As with the other mini-sessions, this short CPD should consist mainly of group discussion, perhaps using think, pair, share to get the ball rolling.

Slide 5: Managing progress

Discussion:

- When students are working independently, what can you do to help them make progress?
- What resources do you need to have in place to support independent learning?

Assessment and evaluation *(Discussion)*

This mini-session is designed to initiate thinking about the role of assessment in supporting independent learning. Ideas of how this works were explored in chapter six; the focus should be on using assessment to support ongoing learning through activities such as project work.

Invite teachers to think about the aspects of tracking progress and providing feedback. There are opportunities here to think about various forms and levels of feedback. It may well be that regular verbal feedback, following short tutorials in which the mentor reviews a draft of a project, forms the central element in the provision of feedback, as well as the student-tracking process. It is worth discussing how best to capture the outcomes from these conversations (on a tracking spreadsheet, for example).

Slide 6: Assessment and evaluation

Discussion:

- What forms of assessment are applicable when students are learning independently?
- How will you use these to track progress and provide feedback to students?

Bibliography and further reading

Black, P. and Wiliam, D. (1990), *Inside the Black Box. Raising Standards through Classroom Assessment*. GL Assessment Ltd.

Britannica Kids (http://kids.britannica.com/)

Claxton, G. (2008), *What's the Point of School? Rediscovering the Heart of Education*. Oxford: Oneworld Publications.

Coe, R., 'Improving Education. A Triumph of Hope over Experience' (www.cem. org/attachments/publications/ImprovingEducation2013.pdf)

CORE (https://core.ac.uk/)

Creative Education, 'Independent Learning: What role does the teacher have to play?' (http://www.creativeeducation.co.uk/blog/independent-learning/)

Dewey, J. (1938), *Experience and Education*. Kappa Delta Pi.

Didau, D. 'Independence versus Independent Learning' (www.learningspy.co.uk/ literacy/independence-vs-independent-learning/)

Fair, F., Haas, L.E., Gardosik, C., Johnson, D., Price, D. and Leipnik, O. (2015), 'Socrates in the schools: Gains at three-year follow-up' (www.ojs.unisa.edu.au/index.php/ jps/article/view/1268/833)

Findlater, S. (2016), *Bloomsbury CPD Library: Marking and Feedback*. London: Bloomsbury.

Friesen, S. and Scott, D., 'Inquiry-Based Learning: A Review of the Research Literature' (www.galileo.org/focus-on-inquiry-lit-review.pdf)

Google Scholar (https://scholar.google.co.uk/)

Hay, S. (2005), 'Seeing Both Sides of an Issue: Teaching an online moral issues course', *Discourse*, 5, (1), 134–141.

Hendrick, C., 'What do we mean by Independent Learning?' (http://learning. wellingtoncollege.org.uk/what-do-we-mean-by-independent-learning/)

Hmelo-Silver, C., Duncan, R. and Chinn, C. (2006), 'Scaffolding and Achievement in Problem-Based and Inquiry Learning: A Response to Kirschner, Sweller, and Clark' (http://www.cogtech.usc.edu/publications/hmelo_ep07.pdf)

Kohn, A., (1999), *The Schools our Children Deserve.* New York, NY: Houghton Mifflin Harcourt.

Kohn, A., 'Blog Posts' (www.alfiekohn.org/blog/)

Kohn, A., 'Who's Asking?' (www.alfiekohn.org/article/questions/)

Langman, P., 'How our college is cultivating independent learning in A level classes' (https://www.theguardian.com/teacher-network/2012/aug/23/ independent-learners-a-level-classroom)

OpenDOAR, 'The Directory of Open Access Repositories' (www.opendoar.org/)

Open University'60 Second Adventures in Thought' (www.youtube.com/playlist?li st=PL73A886F2DD959FF1)

Plato, *Meno* (http://classics.mit.edu/Plato/meno.html)

Playfair, E., 'Promoting a sixth form student research culture' (https:// eddieplayfair.com/2014/09/02/promoting-a-sixth-form-student-research-culture/)

Taylor, J. (2012), *Think Again: A Philosophical Approach to Teaching*. London: Bloomsbury.

Taylor. J., 'From Monologue to Dialogue: Promoting Learning Through Classroom Discussion' (https://www.cranleigh.org/our-school/ academics/academic-enrichment/learning-and-teaching/blog/ monologue-dialogue-promoting-learning-classroom-discussion/)

Willingham, D., 'What will improve a student's memory?' (https://www.aft.org/ sites/default/files/periodicals/willingham_0.pdf)

Worley, P. (2010), *The If Machine: Philosophical Enquiry in the Classroom*. London: Continuum.

Worley, P., 'The Question X revisited' (https://philosophyfoundation.wordpress.com/tag/closed-questions/)

Index